Partners in Grace

Partners in Grace

Friends of the Salty Saints

MICHEAL ELLIOTT

The Pilgrim Press
Cleveland, Ohio

The Pilgrim Press, Cleveland, Ohio 44115
© 1992 by Micheal Elliott

Will D. Campbell, *Forty Acres and a Goat* (Atlanta: Peachtree Publishers,
1986), p. 51 and adapted story used by permission

Biblical quotations are from the Revised Standard Version of the Bible,
© 1946, 1952, and 1971 by the Division of Christian Education
of the National Council of the Churches of Christ in the U.S.A.,
and are used by permission.

Printed in the United States of America
The paper used in this publication is acid free and meets the minimum
requirements of American National Standard for Information
Sciences-Permanence of Paper for Printed Library Materials,
ANSI Z39.48-1984

97   96   95   94   93   92   5   4   3   2   1

Library of Congress Cataloging-in-Publication Data

Elliott, Micheal, 1956–
    Partners in grace : friends of the salty saints / Micheal Elliott.
        p. cm.
    ISBN 0-8298-0939-2
    1. Church work with the homeless. 2. Meditations.   I. Title.
BV4456.E45 1992
261.8'325—dc20   91-38005
                                                     CIP

To
Vernon Robertson, a father,
Claude Drouet, a brother,
and Cindy Bucy, a sister

Like good stewards of the manifold grace of God, serve one another with whatever gift each of you has received.

—1 Peter 4:10

Contents

Preface   9

Introduction   13

PART ONE:
PARTNERS IN FAITH

1   Banking on Faith   18

2   Where Is Church?   23

3   Spiritual Schizophrenia   27

4   Faith in Numbers   31

5   Financing by Faith   35

6   The Task of Making God Exist (Jer. 22:13–17)   39

PART TWO:
PARTNERS IN HOPE

7   The Business of Caring   46

8   The Magdalene Project   50

9   Underdressed with Someplace to Go   54

10   One Neighbor at a Time   58

11   The Breakfast Club   64

12   Answers We Already Know (Luke 10:20–28)   69

PART THREE:
PARTNERS IN LOVE

13 **The Father of the Homeless**   *76*

14 **A Prodigal Son's Father**   *80*

15 **Friends Who Know**   *84*

16 **Living through "Love"**   *89*

17 **Rediscovering Love**   *93*

18 **Why Love the Poor? (James 2:5–7)**   *97*

PART FOUR:
PARTNERS IN DOUBT

19 **A Broken Family Tree**   *104*

20 **Old Clothes**   *109*

21 **Sleeping Over**   *113*

22 **Used Food**   *117*

23 **A Deadly Dream**   *122*

24 **The Liberation of a Dream (Isaiah 58:4–8)** *126*

PART FIVE:
PARTNERS IN GRACE

25 **The Gift of the Poor**   *134*

26 **Giving Thanks**   *139*

27 **The Ministry of Political Football**   *142*

28 **Token Prayers**   *146*

29 **The Gift of Children**   *150*

30 **Roll Away the Stone (Mark 16:1ff.)**   *153*

References Cited   *159*

Preface

THE STORY BEHIND THESE STORIES began several years ago with *The Society of Salty Saints*, a collection much like this one. It told the story of a ragtag inner-city congregation that, in spite of everything going against them, strove to make a difference. After leaving that church, I walked out into the streets, grew depressed at the homeless poverty there, and wrote *The Community of the Abandoned*. On the streets, however, I noticed the buildings on either side, occupied by bankers, stockbrokers, lawyers, and other such people I really did not know. While one foot was firmly planted in the street, the other strayed into these homes and offices, and much to my surprise, I found these people struggling with issues of faith and lack of faith. *Partners in Grace* is about some of the people I met off the streets.

They see the homeless from their car windows as they drive to work and from time to time actually encounter the poor in the streets. I found again I learned a great deal from people from whom I did not expect to learn. I am struck that grace occurs in the least likely places. The things they had to say have become important to me and merit retelling.

As Robert Coles wrote, "The people who come to see us bring their stories. They hope they tell them well enough so that we understand the truth of their lives. They know how to interpret their stories correctly. We have to remember that what we hear is their story" (*The Call of Stories*, p. 7). I would only add that sometimes their stories become our stories too. Sometimes this is because we are a part of their stories. Other times it is because their stories affect our lives, teaching us new lessons or breaking down old stereotypes.

These stories are as true as my memory serves me. Some facts are too painful for me to remember clearly, so I am sure that by some defense mechanism they were somehow changed as I internalized them. Others are as true as the version they told.

The Scripture passages cited are ones the stories brought to mind, and the prayers, which are the most honest part of the book, are my personal reactions to the lessons learned.

After living these stories, then writing them down and discovering others might be interested in reading them, I put them in book form. I am reminded of a line from the song "Incommunicado" by Jimmy Buffett: "After that last line, I put the book by itself on the shelf with my heart in it."

Some special people who have been significant instruments of grace in my life merit special attention, although God sends so many my way I could not possibly mention them all. The friends who work with me on a daily basis — Dianne Reel Fuller, Karen Jack, Rodger Pack, Michelle Washington, Brandie Haywood, Susan Watts, Clayton Hysell, Michael Freeman, Jay Davis, and Amanda McClain — all challenge and sustain me at the shelters. Joe Daniel (who can take a joke), Richard Moore, Mary Cann, Elizabeth Sprague, John Ferguson, and the other members of the Board of Directors of Union Mission, Inc., make my work more enjoyable and, I hope, more professional. Former board member Frank Stanton is a friend who reminds me when it is time to get away and who helps make it possible, who always has an ear to lend, and who even coins phrases that become titles of books. Gwen and Edward Dukes look after me and make certain I have coffee in the mornings. Our friends across town, John Finney, Terry Tolbert, Lenora Broome, Janet Lee, and Beverly Williams, are partners in poverty. Our friends in the shelters,

Cathy Schmitz, Wes Johnson, and Melinda Pipen, help us do what we do. Gaye Smith, Mary Ann Beile, Bill Broker (I really didn't do it), Rabbi Saul Rubin, Sidney Daniel, and Jamie Maury make me laugh and brighten many gloomy days. Fred Andrea, who tries to be my minister, is a gift.

My Aunt "Bootsie" cuts my hair and sings me songs. Terry Ball, who gives money away for a living, lends me things to read I normally would never consider. William and Bootsie Shearhouse and their son Bill are wonderful hosts in Athens. My dear friends Guy and Anita Sayles, Bill and Kathy Berry, and Wayne Anderson gracefully call just when I need them. Billy, Margaret, David, and Angie continue to love and support me. Rev. Ira and Edith Carver are wonderful grandparents. The folks at the Breakfast Club on Tybee Island — Jody, Bruce, Val, Lori, Kathleen, Clair, and Mr. Jake — start many days off right, and Kenny and Elaine Williams keep the conversation going.

More than these, however, are Janice, Jeremy, Kristen, and Chelsea — the loves of my life. Regardless of where we have lived, they make it home, and they are the greatest gift of grace God has given to me. Without them, I would be adrift at sea with little hope of ever finding my way home again.

Introduction

AS THE DIRECTOR OF A SHELTER FOR THE HOMELESS, I live in two different worlds. One is the world of the poor. The homeless, those dying with AIDS, the substance abuser, the working mother, the underemployed — all encounter me on a daily basis. These teach me great lessons of faith, hope, love, doubt, and grace.

When Hurricane Hugo was sixty miles offshore and it was still not determined if it would make landfall at Savannah, Georgia, or Charleston, South Carolina, I worked frantically at the Grace House, a shelter for the homeless, trying to find appropriate accommodations for the hundreds of homeless men, women, and children fleeing the heavy winds and rain. Earlier in the day, I had sent my wife and children further inland, and now as the afternoon slipped away and Hugo inched closer to land, I was getting regular calls from my wife telling me to leave. The homeless staff employed at the shelter heard me tell her that I could not yet go. Too many people were still coming and I knew they would continue to come. Many would not have heard the news and had no idea of the additional danger of remaining on the streets. The professional staff had all left. I could not leave; I had to be at the shelter.

We continued to tape windows, stock the supply cabinets with food, check batteries for the flashlights and send busloads of homeless people to the Red Cross emergency shelters set up throughout the county. My wife continued to call, demanding that I leave. The news continued to call for the evacuation of

13

areas across the city. The hurricane continued to move closer to land.

As I dashed inside, after making sure the latest bus was completely filled, several of the homeless staff and volunteers stopped me.

"Why don't you leave? Your wife is worried sick about you. We can handle things here." Their faces were full of concern and compassion for me.

"No, I can't. There's too much to do. We know that a lot of people will not come inside until tonight. They have no idea that the hurricane is coming. No matter how many we ship off, the shelter will still be full tonight."

"It's okay," they replied. "We can handle it."

"No, I'm supposed to be here. It's my job."

I went back to the task at hand. I was dumbfounded, however, that our roles were reversing. I was at Grace House to take care of the homeless. Now they were trying to take care of me.

My wife called again and demanded that I leave at that very moment. I told her it wouldn't be much longer. When I hung up, they gathered around me again.

"Look, you have a family to take care of. Your wife is worried sick about you. We don't have a family. We'll take care of the shelter. You take care of them."

I was caught in the middle of my obligation to my family and my calling to the homeless. I wanted to leave. I was as frightened as anyone else. I wanted to remain, too. I was supposed to be the one administering grace. The shoe was suddenly on the other foot. So we sat and planned what would be done, and I left.

According to Frederick Buechner, "Grace is something you can never get but only be given. There's no way to earn it or deserve it or bring it about any more than you can deserve the taste of raspberries and cream or earn good looks or bring about your own birth" (*Wishful Thinking*, p. 33). I knew what he meant. Somehow I was no longer the minister, but the one being ministered to. The homeless and the poor have taught me more about grace than anyone else.

My other world, however, is that of everyday America. I know bankers, housewives, politicians, homebuilders, company executives, clergy, and members of the Junior League. I go to dinner parties in their homes, receive their phone calls asking what they can do to help, and sit in their offices asking for money to continue the shelter operation. Many have become my friends.

As these relationships flourished, I began to notice the intense interest that many of the non-homeless have in matters of faith, hope, love, doubt, and grace. I observed how the world of the homeless affected them. It changed the way I thought about the "rich," because I had fallen into the trap of loving the poor by hating the rich. I learned that the same grace the poor and the homeless had presented me with was offered by these newfound friends. Robert McAfee Brown calls this grace "creative surprise":

> A stranger walks into one's life and a friendship abides; a chance encounter is the initiation of a series of planned encounters and a marriage of thirty-six years' duration results; a piece of music is first heard by the chance spinning of a radio dial or a randomly selected phonograph record or because someone happened to play that piece and not another — and it becomes an instrument of healing in subsequent times of spiritual fever. (*Creative Dislocation — The Movement of Grace*, p. 80)

I have found that the homeless experience produces a great wealth of God's grace for those who seek to struggle with it. I have found much grace in my relationships with the poor and the homeless and have written of these twice before. As the circle of relationships that I have made grows wider, however, I find that the grace of "creative surprise" does too. Members of the Junior League begin to challenge my stereotypes where the homeless used to. Bankers teach me a great deal about the struggle for faith. Wealthy men and women renew my sense of hope that the world can be what God intended it to be. Company executives confront me with grace. Suddenly, I realize the community of believers is not as narrow as I thought. The number of those willing to struggle with the demands of the Gospel is greater than I once believed. Now I feel the world is not quite as lost as I used to.

This is the celebration of lessons learned from new friends who are not homeless and poor. Most have shown me the grace to enter into a country that is foreign to me. They have accepted me where I am and allowed me to cross over into their homes. These partners in grace make the struggle bearable, the doubts endurable, and the journey entertaining. When Paul ended his famous discourse on love in 1 Corinthians, he said, "But now abide faith, hope, love, these three; but the greatest of these is love." I do not doubt this. Even so, while love may be the greatest, grace is the most fun.

PART ONE

Partners in Faith

HAVING FAITH IN GOD is a lot like having faith in your best friends. When the times are good we need someone to celebrate with and when the times are bad we need someone's shoulder to cry on. Good friends can be counted on in either situation. We do the same with God, of course, whispering quick prayers of thanksgiving when we get what we want or petitions of intervention when we do not. God, however, usually leaves it to our friends to vouch for heavenly interest in our affairs and chooses to keep quiet, personally keeping a distance.

Certainly there are those times when God seems to be pulling us along. Our friends are keeping the distance, and people we barely know are the ones speaking the loudest. These are the times that confuse us the most and leave us shaking our heads in wonder. We do not see very far ahead and ask where in the world God is.

There are times, though, when God speaks loud and clear through the voice of others. Unfortunately, most of us would rather be addressed directly, even though God is obviously more comfortable delegating joyous exclamations or tear-stained shoulders to others.

17

— 1 —

Banking on Faith

HE DOES NOT ACT like a bank executive is supposed to act. In the plush surroundings of the trust department, where offices have a hushed and sepulchral flavor of money, the ceilings are high, the carpeting deep, the paneling dark and glossy and curved, John spits his chewing tobacco into a paper cup. Through trial and error, with an excellent sense of how to make money work, motivated by a strong work ethic, he has worked his way up to a position of prestige. People who know John claim that he is not as wild as he used to be. He no longer drinks or runs naked on roof tops, but he still retains a sense of humor and a biting wit, and he loves to pull off a mean practical joke. His superiors have often attempted to instruct him on how to act at work. They tell him that he is not to chew tobacco at work or tell off-color jokes, and he smiles nicely and continues to be nothing other than who he is.

John was born and raised in South Georgia, attended a southern college, married young, and always worked hard. Once while still at Mercer University, a friend whose family lived near John's asked him for a ride home. Friday, after classes were over, they piled into John's car and made their way to a sleepy little community outside Americus, Georgia.

"What kind of place is this?" John asked.

"Uh, it's a Christian community," the friend replied. "It's interracial. My daddy runs it. It's called Koinonia."

"What's that?"

"It's the Greek word for fellowship."

John was intrigued. He spent most of the afternoon meeting the people who lived in this community, observing their peanut farms, and hearing about the sometimes violent racist attitudes that people in nearby Americus held for Koinonia. It was almost dark by the time John left and he still had a long drive ahead. When he got home, his father demanded to know where John had been. When John told him, he exploded with anger and told his son that he was never to go to such a nigger-loving place again.

Years later, John began to grow more concerned with the issues of faith in his life. He left the Baptist church he was raised in, became a Methodist, and was very active in the new congregation. He ceased running with his old buddies and joined the board of directors of a Christian school and of a homeless shelter. He spent more time in his garden and reading religious books. He still chewed tobacco at the bank and drove his old red pickup truck, but he settled down as much as possible.

One evening he volunteered to attend a worship service at the shelter. The members of the board of directors were encouraged to attend at least one service a month. John arrived on time and took his seat amid homeless men and women who had gathered to worship. The leaders for the night's service were from the Bible Chapel, a nearby black congregation who had expressed concern for the homeless since the shelter had first opened.

The worship was a celebration of the fact that people had been able to serve. They gave thanks to God for being able to live through another day, for being able to eat and sleep in the shelter that night, and for all the bountiful blessings that the Lord continued to bestow upon them. They sang songs, clapped their hands, and spent a lot of time hugging in Christian fellowship. When each of the participants was given the opportunity to testify, John was struck that so many of the homeless offered thanks and praise to God for all that had been done for them. He knew that many had nothing but the clothes on their backs and a few coins in their pockets, yet they still praised God. He thought of everything that he owned — the house outside the city, all his friends, and the money that was tucked away in the bank for when he needed it. A lump rose in his throat as he joined in the fellowship and became an active worshipper with the ragtag congregation.

In the months that followed, two area ministers began to criticize the shelter because it did not conduct mandatory worship services. They claimed that a Christian shelter should make everyone attend worship services in return for food and shelter. John replied he never read that Jesus made the five thousand listen to his sermon before he fed them fish and bread. It had no effect on the clergy, however, and they continued to call publicly for actions against the shelter. After several months of bad publicity, a meeting was called between all the persons involved.

After beginning with prayer and Bible readings, the clergy attacked the shelter for not acting like an extension of the church, for taking government funds, for having a Jewish secretary, and for posting nonreligious quotations throughout the building. The staff tried to defend their actions, asking if the clergy forced those people they visited to attend Sunday services. When the clergy replied that they did not, they were asked if the homeless had the same right to attend only if they wanted.

They asked John how he stood in all of this. John cleared his throat and spoke softly, but passionately. "I'm not a minister, but I know that the spirit of God is at the shelter. We have worship services and the homeless attend them. I participate in them on a regular basis."

His eyes filled with mist and his voice cracked as he continued. "In those services, the homeless praise God for all that has been done for them. They express thanks for the shelter, the staff, the opportunities presented to them. They are happy because they do not have to spend another night outside, have food in their stomachs, and the chance to start over again the next day. I don't think that God intends us to make anyone worship him, but I do know that it happens freely and honestly at the shelter. They have faith that I don't have. They can still praise God when they don't have much of anything. I wish that my faith was as strong."

The clergy were caught off guard for a moment. They had counted on John's traditional views to support their arguments. After only a moment of silence, however, they picked up where they had left off, growing even louder and more convinced that they were right.

As we left the meeting, John stuffed his mouth with tobacco and said, "Let's get back to work."

For indeed we have had the Good News preached to us, just as they also; but the word they heard did not profit them, because it was not united by faith in those who heard.

— Hebrews 4:2

God who is faithful to me,
who continues to present the Gospel to me,
offering me new opportunities every day
to be challenged in my faith,
to grow in my convictions,
and to experience the good news of the Gospel
where I least
expect to see it,
remain near me always.
For I find that my faith
leads me away from the familiar
to face new people
and different ideas.
I find that change is always difficult,
and often frightening,
pulling me along behind when I do not really want to follow.
Yet, O Lord,

I find myself assured that the world I hope for,
the world that you prepared for me,
is one where men and women accept one another
for who they are,
without trying to make them into something
you never intended them to be.
Help me O God,
to always be
what you created me to be.
Nothing more,
and nothing less.

— 2 —

Where Is Church?

During a drive after a speaking engagement in Memphis, Tennessee, I decided to stop in Nashville, call Will Campbell, and see if he was free for a visit. Will is the closest thing Southern Baptists have to an Old Testament prophet and is well known for his writings and preaching. I finally found a phone across the street from Barbara Mandrel's museum and dialed the number. Will answered, told me to come on, and gave me a page full of directions. An hour of wrong turns later, I parked beside the small log cabin that serves as his office, behind the white frame house he lives in with his wife, Brenda. Stretching after the drive, I looked at his yard and was struck by an impressive row of bamboo that stood some fifteen feet tall.

Will invited me in, taking the time from pecking on an old beat-up typewriter, spit a mouthful of tobacco juice into a brass spittoon, leaned back in his chair, and freely gave me all the time we needed. We caught one another up on mutual friends, talked about Clarence Jordan and the recent passing away of his wife, Florence, and Will's latest book. Inevitably the conversation turned to theology and the role of the church in the world today.

"Will, do you go to church?" I asked.

"All the time," he replied as he wiped mud from his cowboy boots. "I find church happens all the time."

"No," I tried to clarify my question. "What do you do on Sunday mornings at eleven o'clock. Do you attend a church service?"

"Oh," he responded, "you mean do I go to those steeples. I thought you wanted to know if I went to church."

"Aren't those steeples church? I know that many don't do the kinds of things churches are supposed to do, but there is still an element of church in them."

"You think so?" he shot back.

"Well, if they're not, I'm not sure I know what church is. I had a friend in seminary who rarely spoke during his three years. One of the last classes everyone has to take prior to graduating deals with exiting seminary and entering the church. On the last day of his last class, the professor, a retired minister himself, asked if anyone had any final words. My quiet friend raised his hand, cleared his throat, and informed the class he thought they had all made a mistake. The churches they were leaving seminary for, and the way they had been prepared to run those churches, was not at all what Jesus had in mind when he started Christian communities. My friend went on to say he thought the best thing they could do for Jesus upon entering their new churches was to rent a bulldozer and level the buildings they were called to minister. Then they could start over and do it the way Jesus probably wanted." I asked Will if this was what he thought.

He did not answer, but stood up and said it was time for lunch. Following behind, he walked across the yard to the white frame house, told Brenda we were going to Gasses, and wanted to know if she wanted to come. She said she did not. Then she told him to stay out of trouble.

We drove several miles until we came to a crossroads with nothing there except a combination gas station, convenience store, and restaurant. We walked inside and saw the place was nearly empty. At one end stood a bar and the rest of the room was filled with tables covered with red and white table cloths. The walls were covered with country music record covers and the bar boasted a cartoon of Will seated at the same bar. We took our seats in the middle of the room and ordered. It was a few minutes before noon.

At twelve o'clock workers entered and filled the tables around us. I wanted to continue our conversation, but could not because one after another came to the table to speak to Will. Most were dressed in dirty work clothes and appeared to be construction workers. One thanked him for performing his sister's wedding. Another reminded Will to visit his mother in the hospital. A third asked Will if he would talk to his wife because they were having problems. They came for most of the hour asking for Will to perform the functions of a minister in their church-less lives. He responded to each as a shepherd overseeing a flock, giving each all the time he needed.

By one o'clock the room was empty again as all the workers hurried out and returned to their jobs. Will silently finished his sandwich. Grabbing the check, he stood up to leave.

"Well," he said, "church is over for today. Let's go home."

And as he sat at table in his house, many tax collectors and sinners were sitting with Jesus and his disciples; for there were many who followed him. And the scribes and the Pharisees, when they saw that he was eating with sinners and tax collectors, said to his disciples, "Why does he eat with tax collectors and sinners?" And when Jesus heard it, he said to them, "Those who are well have no need of a physician, but those who are sick; I came not to call the righteous, but sinners."

— Mark 2:15–17

> *Do you not know that you are God's Temple and that God's spirit dwells in you? ...For God's Temple is holy, and that Temple you are.*

— 1 Corinthians 3:16–17

I often find, O Lord,
that I am uncertain of what it means
to be one of the sheep in your flock.
Too often,
when I go to my church,
I am surrounded by people who are not sick,
or who have only minor ailments.
When I leave my church
too often I am aware
that my needs have not been met,
that only superficial fellowship was attained,
and that my commitment is more to an institution
that is more concerned with buildings, budgets,
proper music, and short sermons,
than it is with eating with sinners
and those who cannot dress up to attend.
And listening to the fine organ play old hymns,
I stare out the stained-glass window
with the plaque praising the name of the donor,
and wonder about all the ones who are outside.
Then I wonder if I'm in the right place.
And as the sermon begins,
I find myself wondering
which side of the stained glass you are on.

— 3 —

Spiritual Schizophrenia

IT HAPPENS ALMOST EVERY TIME I give a speech or sermon to a church group. When I am shaking hands after the service, someone comes to me, offers greetings, and tells me words I have come to hate. This time was no different. I was in Knoxville, Tennessee, preaching a sermon on missions. It was a huge white church on a lovely lawn that hid the concrete parking lot. The pastor was out of town, which is usually the case when I am invited to preach, so the minister of music was acting as host. The sermon had centered on the biblical mandate to love God by loving others, especially the poor, and starting with one another. It was no different from many of the sermons I preach.

After I finished, though, when the invitation hymn was being sung and the congregation was shifting uncomfortably from one foot to the other, a woman left her seat and stood behind the pulpit. Since this was not a part of the normal Sunday morning routine, everyone appeared confused. She was young, pretty, and in tears. Silently, she waited until she could speak. After a while, the music ceased, but the congregation remained standing holding their open hymnbooks.

"I hope you were listening to this man," she told her church. "He was telling us things we needed to hear."

Her voice was trembling, but she spoke with conviction. Tears continued to stream down her face. Looking into the congregation, I saw everyone's attention was on what she was saying.

"For too long now, we have simply been going along, doing the same things, week in and week out.... We take care of the building, we take care of the service, making sure it is what we want it to be. But we don't take care of each other! And we certainly don't take care of all of those hurting around us! Every year we complain we are losing members, but we aren't doing anything to reach out to the new people who move into the neighborhood because they are poor and black. This isn't what the Gospel says to do...."

She said other things, but I do not think anyone heard her. The minister of music moved behind her and she must have sensed it. The congregation began to stir again with uneasiness. She continued crying when the organist resumed playing the invitation hymn. No one made a decision during the verses that were sung so the service ended as it normally did. Now, standing beside my host, shaking the hands of the congregation, I wondered what had happened.

A middle-aged woman held my hand, told me she had enjoyed the service, and told me that it had been the wife of the minister of youth who had spoken after me. She apologized and said she hoped I wasn't offended. Then she said the words:

"I am so glad," she began, "that you are called to do what you do. I certainly couldn't do it, but I am so comforted to know God calls people like you. You are so special and you have that special calling."

I always feel strange when I hear words like these. I don't feel particularly special in working with the sick, the poor, and the homeless. In fact, I feel anyone can do what I do.

"Do you mean," I responded, "that you do not feel you could do the things I do?"

"No," she smiled, "my calling is different from yours."

"Really! How is it different?"

"My calling is in the church, not outside of it."

"I didn't know there was such a calling. Can I ask you something? What happens when you're the only one around and a homeless person asks you for help? What would you do if a man with AIDS asked you to help him?"

"I'd call the preacher," she replied.

"What if the preacher were not available?"

She looked as if she had been painted into a corner. A frown replaced the smile and I thought she was getting angry. I told her I was not trying to be difficult, but wanted to know how she would apply her faith when confronted with a need, especially if a specialist were not around.

"A specialist?" she asked.

"Does it seem to you," I continued, "that the church hires people to do the things the typical member does not care for? Like loving people different from us? Or caring for people who frighten us? I only wonder how you would handle it?"

"That's why," she cheerfully concluded, "we have missionaries."

Afterward, the church leadership took us to lunch. The conversation was strained as the minister of youth's wife was present and no one seemed to want to discuss the mission of the church. I felt like I had said everything I should and ate silently. I was asked about the long aisle discussion I had with the woman called to sustain the church. I told them we had talked about missions.

During the long drive home that afternoon, I wondered about that church. Specifically, I wondered what the minister would be told when he returned. I was sure that he would be preaching a series on the mission of the church before too long.

If a brother or a sister is ill-clad and in lack of daily food, and one of you says to them, "Go in peace, be warmed and filled," without giving them the things needed for the body, what does it profit? So faith itself, if it has no works, is dead."

—James 2:26–27

God who calls us all,
who plainly states the business
your followers are to be about,
and who says time and again in your word,
to love the poor and the sick,
to care for those who are without,
and to be willing to meet people where they are,
why do so many have a spiritual schizophrenia
when they seek to live out their faith?
How can so many
divorce their spiritual life
from their day-to-day living?
Is not the example Jesus set plain?
Doesn't your written word spell it out?
It is no wonder
so many are hurting
and so few are helping.
It is also no wonder
when someone calls Christians to be uncomfortable,
the words are dismissed or minimized.
Worship is allowed to continue
while wounded people walk outside,
rarely daring to come in.

— 4 —

Faith in Numbers

HOWARD IS A MEMBER OF THE BOARD OF DIRECTORS. Unlike many who serve in such a capacity, he is also one of the volunteers at the shelter. Once every week he arrives at 3:30 in the afternoon to assist in checking the homeless into the shelter. His role is to greet everyone, document their stay, determine if they are first-time guests or not, fill out intake forms if they are, and help shepherd the homeless for another night of warehouse living. He has learned that homeless shelters really are a poor substitute for a home. Howard managed a parts warehouse before retirement.

He is a man of deeply felt religious conviction and this is his primary motivation to serve. Opening the shelter had been a difficult experience for the board of directors. When they were first approached about doing it, most felt they were too old.

"If we're going to do something like this," one remarked, "we have to get some new blood. We're all too old."

Several new board members were brought on, all men and all white. After all, this is south Georgia. To their credit, however, they continued to press for the creation for a new homeless shelter. The money was raised, a site was secured, and a press conference was held to announce their intentions to the community. The community surrounding the proposed site rallied together, chose leaders, and announced it did not want "that kind of people in our neighborhood," an objection expressed in several ways:

- "Our community is a nice place to live. We recognize there is a homeless problem, and we hope something will be done to help these people, but not in this neighborhood."

- "The homeless are mostly mentally ill and drug users. We don't want that kind of people around our children."

- "We've seen the homeless lying around and sleeping in bushes. This is a pretty neighborhood. We have some of the nicest parks in the city. We don't want people lying in our bushes."

- "The homeless problem is downtown, not here. If something is to be done, then let it be done downtown."

- "If the homeless locate in our community, think about what it would do to our property value."

The complaints were endless, and after just a short while it became apparent to the members of the board of directors that the neighborhood group was too powerful. So they announced that another site would be chosen. But the same rejection occurred on four separate occasions. The members of the board of directors learned first hand about the "not-in-my-backyard" syndrome.

After two years of trying to secure the right site, city officials finally stepped in and announced they would assist in negotiating the appropriate location. In the end, the right site turned out to be behind the bus station and next to the city's largest public housing project. Unlike the "nicer" communities, the poor welcomed the homeless with open arms. The housing project hosted a fried chicken dinner and invited anyone who was homeless to attend. No one from the other communities supported this effort.

Since the controversy had ended, Howard was content to make a difference by helping to operate the shelter one night each week. Seated at the check-in desk, he did his best to welcome the homeless and make certain the paperwork was filled out appropriately. The shelter had remained filled to capacity throughout the first winter and most of the members of the board were pleased to help meet such a huge need.

On the first warm day of spring, Howard took his normal seat at the check-in desk. He greeted everyone by commenting on the beautiful day. No one could argue. It had been a wonderful warm afternoon. After a few hours, however, Howard was concerned so few homeless people were checking into the shelter. Normally, by six o'clock all the beds were filled. On this night, only about half were occupied.

"This is terrible," he commented. "I would hate to see this place go unused. What would we do with this place if only a few homeless people came here every day? This is a big building to fill. Where is everyone?"

One of the staff sat next to him. "Don't worry, Howard. They'll be back."

"I'd just hate to think about what we'd do if we discovered we had more building than we really need."

"Actually," came the reply, "it would be kind of nice. It would mean homelessness is going away. We would not have to warehouse people for a living anymore. They could all find their own housing. If homelessness did go away, there would be another purpose for the building. I'm sure the homeless enjoyed the day and want to enjoy the evening too."

"You think so?" Howard asked.

"Sure, and homelessness won't go away any time soon." The voice was sad: "Jesus said the poor would be with us always."

Howard sat silent for a few moments before speaking. "Yes, he did. I never thought of it that way before."

"Didn't you have faith that when you opened this place, it was for the right reason?"

"I thought I did," he replied.

Since that night, the shelter has rarely had an empty bed.

If you want to be happy, be kind to the poor; it is a sin to despise anyone.

—Proverbs 14:21

Speak up for people who cannot speak for themselves. Protect the rights of all who are helpless. Speak for them and be a righteous judge. Protect the rights of the poor and needy.

—Proverbs 31:8–9

O God, why am I sometimes so concerned
with the amount of good works
more than I am with the work itself?
Why am I preoccupied with numbers
rather than the joy of helping?
Why do I define success in numerical terms
rather than with a spiritual definition?
I notice, Lord,
too many of your followers
count your sheep.
If they are so busy counting them,
when do they feed them?
Numbers can mislead me, Lord.
A lot means I am doing good.
A few mean I have fallen short.
Numbers can also intimidate me, Lord.
When I look at the mass of poor and needy people,
people who need me,
I despair because there are too many.
Numbers can confuse me too, Lord.
You walk away from ninety-nine
and go off searching for one,
but I concede the loss and tend what is left.
Help me learn to count, Lord,
as you do.

— 5 —

Financing by Faith

SEVERAL YEARS AGO, when I served as pastor of an inner-city congregation, I was host to one of the many church groups that would take a mission trip downtown. They were from the suburbs and, having read about the needs of the homeless and the poor, they sought somehow to live out the Gospel by driving the church bus downtown. If they were impressed enough by the ministries, we had been told, they would make a significant contribution. Financing by faith is tough on anyone; we needed their money.

Arriving at the church, they were mostly well-dressed women led by the pastor's wife. She was an attractive woman who, like Tammy Fay Baker, wore more make-up than she did clothes. She led the women up the stairs while she continued to lecture them on the differences between liberals and true believers. Standing off to one side, I listened to her monologue.

"Liberals call themselves moderates," she was saying, "in some silly attempt to fool us, but we know about them. They minimize the importance of preaching the Gospel to the lost. Most of the time, they are more concerned about good works than about proclaiming the Word of God. Of course, it is easy to understand how they could be so confused. They do not believe that the Bible is the inerrant and infallible written word of God."

There was a time when I placed myself squarely in the "moderate" camp, but that was before I learned it was easier to get many conservative churches to respond to the poor simply by pointing out that the Bible spends more time commanding Christians to care for the poor than almost anything else. These congregations do not really care for biblical mandates about inviting the homeless into our homes or how much the Lord judges in favor of the oppressed, but when it is pointed out that the Bible says it, they have to believe it and that, more or less, settles it. On the other hand, "moderate" churches say all the right things about being a force for justice and having concern for the poor, but most of what they do is token. While her discourse would have bothered me at one time, it no longer did.

When she finished, I was introduced to her group and told I could begin. Leading them throughout the building, I described all the ministries that took place. It was not long, however, before they stopped me and asked one question that was on their minds.

"Where are the rats?" the pastor's wife asked.

"I beg your pardon," I replied, certain I did not hear the question correctly.

"Where are the rats?" she asked again. "There are always rats in the inner city. This building is too clean. It doesn't look like an inner-city church is supposed to look."

Since that time, I have encountered many such people who, when they tour the shelter, want to know why it is so clean, why there are no rats, and why it doesn't look like the starving country of Ethiopia has moved inside one building. I try to explain that just because people are poor doesn't mean they are dirty, and simply because a building exists primarily for the poor doesn't mean it has to look like an indoor landfill. Too often, though, reality is so far from their stereotypes that they are unable to comprehend anything else I have to say.

Those who do become involved, however, typically run into other difficulties. After the initial baptism into the world of ministry in poverty, they inevitably criticize the shelter in one of two ways. First, they say, I attempt to do too much too fast. It is true, of course. Because there is so much need in the world and because the Bible is pretty plain about responding to needs whenever they are encountered, I move quickly to put need, volunteers, and money together to meet that need. Since there is always more need than there are volunteers and money, I do what I can and pray that God will move others to deliver on the resources. Most of the time, God does. It makes everyone uncomfortable, however, because financing by faith rarely leaves much of a balance.

The other criticism is that I am not religious enough. What they mean, I think, is that I often do not look or sound religious. This, too, is true. I firmly believe that demonstration of the Gospel is more important than proclamation. It means more to show people that you love them than to tell them. The verbal presentation always comes, but it is after I have tried to show them how much God loves them before I tell them.

Despite having to face the same criticism time and time again, I find it worthwhile. There are times, though, when I wish I did have rats running around the shelter and that the building looked as bad as some wish. It might mean people would contribute more. The ministry might not work as well, but at least the budget would always be in the black.

Lord, I know that you defend the cause of the poor and the rights of the needy.

—Psalm 140:12

God who expresses special love for the poor,
why is it so difficult for us to love them too?
Why do we minimize their struggles,
calling them lazy bums,
convinced they are winos?
Why is it so hard for us
to love them
in the same way we so easily love

those who are not poor?
Why do so many choose to ignore
all the things you mandate us to do for the poor
in your written word?
We never seem to get around to it,
because we are forever trying
to distinguish the "truly" poor
from the fakes.
Forgive us, Lord,
for letting prejudice get in the way
of living proclamations of the Gospel.
Forgive us for forgetting
that you came to bring Good News to the poor,
and that you never seemed to worry about
how you would pay for it.
You simply did it.

— 6 —

The Task of Making God Exist
(Jeremiah 22:13–17)

BILLY TURNER IS NOT A CHRISTIAN ANYMORE. Certainly some
will claim "once saved, always saved," but since I don't worry
much about theology, I'll leave it to them. It is a shame about
Billy. He was doing well. I don't really recall how we first met; I
think he just showed up for breakfast at the shelter one morning,
he stayed for a worship service, and he kept coming.

He was a huge man, weighing at least 350 pounds. He explained his obesity to me. "I grew up during the war. Every night
my mother would fill my plate and tell me, 'Son, don't leave
anything. Every time you leave something on your plate, you're
wasting food and feeding Hitler.' Hell, I tried to starve the entire
German army." Then he slapped me on the back and laughed
until long after any humor had passed from the moment.

He grew up in Paduca, Kentucky, and was proud of it. "Whenever I get myself straightened out," he would say, "I'm going
back."

Sometimes, he and I would sit on the steps, sipping coffee and
talking. He would tell me all about Paduca.

"The best place to eat is a place called Skinheads. It ain't nothing fancy, just good country cooking. Ol' Skinhead is as bald as an egg and every Friday night he gets just as cracked."

Again he would slap me hard on the back, making me spill my coffee, and laugh until the humor was gone. He liked his own jokes best.

From time to time we talked about God and religion, mostly when he brought it up. These conversations did not have great depth to them, just what he thought and what I believed. It was with some surprise, then, when he told me he had been saved. I told Billy that I was glad he joined the church.

"Me, too," he responded, "but can you tell me what I should do with my green stamps?"

"Green stamps?" I asked.

"Yeah, the preacher said the church passed out redemption. I figured it was a redemption center and I want to redeem my green stamps." Again he slapped me on the back and laughed for too long.

He went on to explain, more seriously, how he wanted a new life and a chance to start over. "It's time I straighten up," he said. "It's time I grew up."

"Grew up?" I asked.

"Yeah, grew up. You know... when I spoke as a child I was a child, but when I became a man, I put away childish things.... I want to grow up."

Over the next several months, Billy did everything he could to "grow up." He attended every church service. He quit listening to country music, telling me this was the ultimate sacrifice, and tuned his radio to a Gospel station. He read his Bible daily and prayed often. He even enrolled in a mail order Bible college. Everyone was proud of him. Then one day, with no warning, he quit and dropped out of sight. No one knew what happened to him. It is not unusual, however, to lose homeless people. One day they disappear and are gone forever.

I ran into him not too long ago. He looked the same, as big as a house, and he told me he was trying to starve the Iraqi army to death. He slapped my back, but did not laugh too long.

"Rev," he said, "you know I really gave it a try."

"I know, Billy."

I believe he really did try. Many people have tried doing the things he did, with great expectations of growing up, only to come up with the same results. People join the church. They pray and attempt to read their Bibles daily. Some even enroll in seminary or a Bible class. They give it their best effort, honestly wanting to become Christians, deeply desiring that God exists for them. In the end, though, they just don't feel whatever it was they were hoping to feel and they give up. Most cannot understand why. Because they do many of the acceptable religious things, they fully expect to feel more religious, but do not. So they quit.

Many claim these people did not pray long enough, that they did not understand what their Bibles said, or that it was the devil who prevented them from feeling God. Friends sometimes say that God is indeed with them, but they do not recognize it. Such explanations mean little, however. John Casanas defines the situation the following way: "There is no need to tell people that God is with them, that God will help them, . . . that God is their friend and will save them." It is only when they experience God with them, only when they perceive God saving them, only when they feel God as their friend that they will know God exists (*The Idols of Death and the God of Life*, p. 113).

The problem so many have is when we attempt to "find God" and invite the Holy Spirit into our hearts. Too often, we try to do it through the experience of others. The first thing we need to understand in our search to make God exist for us is that we cannot live vicariously on the experiences and formulas of others. Someone else's experiences are not our experiences. Yet too many pilgrims seek to live out their faith by experiencing God vicariously through another's journey. We listen to religious songs that praise the Lord, but we never actually praise God. We read the powerful testimonies of others, but the lessons learned are never directly applied to our own lives. We learn interpretations and doctrines that others have formed without ever learning our own. We surround ourselves with religious artifacts without ever getting religious. In the end, we must come to the recognition that "knowledge" of God cannot be capitalized on, transferred, or sold. Nor can it be taught. God has to be experienced, and we each must experience God for ourselves if we are to know that God exists.

Too many have developed a "bootleg" faith, feeling that if they act religious enough, singing songs, praying prayers, reading the Bible, and so forth, God will somehow rub off on them. They trust that the experiences of others will get them close enough to catch hold of just enough faith for God to exist in their lives. Just as fool's gold is not the real thing even though it may appear to be, "fool's faith" is not the real thing either. Such faith is rooted in religious activity and not in God. For a while such people may think they have something by acting religious, but in the end they find it is just an act.

Others believe that if they ignore doubts and continue to tell themselves that God is in heaven and all is right with the world, sooner or later they will convince themselves. These believe the goal of faith is religious salvation and, therefore, seek to save the entire world. If enough people are convinced, they convince themselves they are not going to hell because they are saving others. By so concentrating on others, they forget about themselves.

If we cannot find God by doing all kinds of religious things, and if we cannot find God by convincing ourselves and everyone else of heavenly existence, how are we really to know God? How is God found? How do we make God exist for us?

When the prophet Jeremiah went to see King Shallum, or Jehoiakim, son of the very godly Josiah, he was not impressed. In fact, Jeremiah, typically, was angry. The king was constructing a new palace. This was not an ordinary run-of-the-mill palace, however, but a spacious one, beyond all normal needs, with picture windows, radiant heating, and elaborate lighting. It was to be a cathedral made with imported cedar and only the rarest and most expensive materials. This was for God, after all, and God deserves the biggest and the best. This made Jeremiah angry. The prophet knew God did not need such an elaborate palace.

The king's excessive taste was not the only reason for his anger, however; Jeremiah did not like the way it was being built either. "The real problem is not only that the end product is *unnecessary,* but that the means of building it are *unjust*" (Robert McAfee Brown, *Unexpected News*, p. 65). Construction was based on unrighteousness and injustice, for Jehoiakim refused to pay the workers. "The king, at the top of the heap," says Brown, "is accumulating even greater goods for himself by exploiting those at the bottom."

Typical of Old Testament prophets, Jeremiah lets the king have it: "Woe to him who builds his palace by unrighteousness!" The king knew he was the target of the curse. Just getting warmed up, Jeremiah asks a scathing question: "Do you think just because you compete in cedar that you are a king?" Is it the house that makes the man? Does the number of possessions define the person? Do buildings lead to admiration, respect, or being a better person?

To drive the point home, Jeremiah compares the king to his father, which is "the type of putdown grown men don't need" (p. 65). Josiah did not care so much for eating and drinking fine food and wine as he did "justice and righteousness." Even the poor and needy loved Josiah. The implication is clear: the difference between a good king and a bad one is what the poor think of you. Jehoiakim emerges a few cuts below his old man in this category, and that alone must have made the king angry enough to rip the prophet's lips off.

But Jeremiah is not through. Coolly, he asks, "All of this doing justice and righteousness, all of this vindicating of the poor and needy, is not this what it means to know me?"

This is the path to personal knowledge of God. To know God

is to do justice and righteousness and to vindicate the poor and needy. Those who do not, do not know God, regardless of how religiously they act. We may know all about God but not know God. God simply does not exist for us. Spending a great deal of time in religious activity, praying, speaking, reading the Bible are not the same as practicing justice and vindicating the poor and needy.

Knowing God does not necessarily mean going to church, listening to religious music, quoting Scripture, or proclaiming the Gospel every opportunity you have to open your mouth. It may include these, as often it should, but to know God, to make God truly exist for you, is to work for those who are without.

This leads back to Billy Turner, I think, or back to what many of us are feeling. Everything Billy did, the praying, the church attendance, the straightening out, and the growing up, he did just for himself. We cannot blame him much for that, though, as most churches today teach such behavior as the way to know God. Congregations today invite those who would know God to come inside, when the prophets call for the opposite. They tell us to go outside and visit the poor and needy, to go where injustice is and make it right. This is how we come to know God. Knowing God is not getting what we want, but giving away what we have. If we wish to know God, then we must hang around the people Jesus hung around with — the poor, the needy, and the outcast.

Too many spend their time and energy doing religious and good things, but still God does not exist for them. They know about God, but they do not know God. Jeremiah says that to know God is to do justice. If you want to know God, then you must get busy. There is much injustice in the world, more, in fact than most can stand. Choose any injustice, begin to work at correcting it, and, surprise, you will meet God. The struggle for faith will then become secondary, because God will be your partner in fighting the injustices in the world.

PART TWO

Partners in Hope

LIFE WOULD BE VERY DEPRESSING WITHOUT HOPE. Life is really little more than moving from hoping for one thing to hoping for another. We hope a friend will call, that we get the job, that the sermon will not be too long, that we win the lottery, that we make the right impression, that our children's lives are better than our own, that we get to know the right people. We hope that better days are coming or that the good times will not end soon. We hope our ships are finally going to come in.

Action is not always associated with hope. Hope is as much an attitude as anything else. Hope provides just enough of whatever it takes to get us through another day. We hope that tomorrow is better than today.

Sometimes, however, someone combines hope with action. The result can be catastrophic. Mountains can, indeed, be moved. Revolutions do begin. Ships can come in. To have hope that is nothing more than an attitude, not married to action, is safer and makes fewer demands on our lives. Whenever we act on hope, there is always the possibility of disappointment. To be sure, the payoffs are enormous, but so are the risks.

— 7 —

The Business of Caring

THE EXPLOSION IN THE NUMBER of homeless women and families with children on the streets of America caught most of us off guard. Still struggling to provide shelter space for homeless men, we were overwhelmed when mothers with babies began to bed down on hard shelter floors. During the first year, there were twenty-five families that came to our shelter. The next year, the number rose to forty-two. In the first quarter of the third year, however, over sixty-one families had sought refuge at the shelter. It was quickly decided that new shelter space had to be made available for them. A fundraising campaign was begun to raise the half million dollars to construct a new facility.

Grant proposals were written to secure government funding. One would be hard pressed to find homeless shelters supported entirely by the church community or even the private sector. Churches, once the sole supporter of charity in this country, abdicated this position during the Great Depression and have never sought to take it back. Mainline American churches have opted for a privatized theology and a narrow view of missions and have put most of their money into their own operations. The private sector has a difficult time deciding which charity to contribute to. There are so many good causes. Partly because of the philosophy of the "ME Generation," private dollars have diminished over the years. But the three sources together — government, church, and private — provide the typical homeless shelter with enough to maintain its operations.

After a few months, it appeared that about one-third of the money for our shelter would come from government sources. The rest would have to come from the private sector. One of the wealthiest men in our community is Frederick West. A religious man, Mr. West is well known for his support of churches and charities. As our fundraising efforts continued, it became clear that he would be one of the most significant contributors.

When most of the money had been raised, Mr. West called me one day to discuss the project. "I've been thinking about this project," he began. "That is a pretty significant amount of money to put into an area that will never realize a return on the investment."

"I'm sorry," I replied. "I'm not sure I understand what you mean."

"Well, let's say the shelter goes out of business, that in a few years this homeless problem goes away. What would happen to the building? What would be the return on the investment? I would hate to see all that money go into a building that would prove useless after the problem had diminished."

I almost dropped the phone. Never in my years as a minister had I been asked such a question. What is the return on the investment of a charitable contribution? I waited a long time before I answered.

"Mr. West, I suppose there are two ways to reply. If you are looking for any kind of financial reward from the investment, there is none. The building will be built; it will be filled with people and located in a poor neighborhood. Should it ever need to be sold, I am sure that it will be at a very depressed price. In this sense, any contribution is a lousy investment. On the other hand, I know that the facility will be completely full of homeless women and children as soon as it is completed. They will be off the streets, receive proper meals, be exposed to quality programs that will assist them in taking advantage of whatever options that are available to them, and be better off because the building is there."

"I understand all that," he said, "but someone needs to think about these things."

"I'm sure someone does, but I don't come at it that way. Too many nights I have stood in the doorway and told a mother with a baby that there was no more space in the shelter. I have had to hand them a paper towel so they could wipe the tears away as they faced a night on the streets."

"Well," Mr. West said slowly, "whenever emotions are a part of the process, inappropriate decisions can be made."

"Yes, sir, I'm sure that they can. It would be worth a great deal of money to me, however, not to have to say no to these families with children."

In the weeks that followed, Mr. West used his position to more than double the amount of government funds made available to the building project. He agreed to donate the rest. While I will still have to tell mothers that there is no room in the shelter, I will not have to do it as much.

And it came to pass that while they were there, the days were completed for her to give birth. And she gave birth to her firstborn son; and she wrapped him in cloths, and laid him in a manger, because there was no room for them at the inn.

—Luke 2:6–7

God of the ones who sleep outside,
I wonder about those who control the houses.
How do they think about the ones on the streets?
How do they view their obligations to those who have little?
I know that you have said
to those who have been given so much
that much will be demanded.

It often seems to me though
that the ones with so much
are the ones who demand much.
They demand returns on their investments.
They demand accountability.
They demand gratitude.
They demand input.
I do not mind that
and I want people to feel good when they give.
It is just that you call for giving to be pure and natural
for those who believe in you,
when, in fact, giving is a constant struggle
that brings questions of how much do I give
and how much do I keep.
As long as you sit in heaven, we can answer how we want to.
Unless that really is you
with the baby in your arms
walking away from the shelter in the night.

— 8 —

The Magdalene Project

THE MAGDALENE PROJECT is an undertaking for the benefit of homeless women and children. The effort began when the Junior League made a commitment of $50,000 as well as twenty-five volunteers over a two-year period. This women's group said they had always had a white glove image and they wanted to change it to a work glove image. When we first decided to approach the League for help, our stereotypes were intact. To be honest, we wanted their money more than we wanted them.

Most homeless shelters rely heavily on grants for operating costs, staff salaries, and other financial obligations. While the ideal is to rely wholly on churches and private donors, this is rarely possible. In fact, most shelters spend as much time researching grants as they do helping the homeless. Of the many grants I have worked on, the Junior League's was the most exhausting. After the initial written application, which is all that the majority of funding organizations call for, we learned we had made the first cut and were only beginning the application process. There would be a series of meetings in which a review committee would learn everything there was to know about the proposal, the need, the organization, and the long-term effects of the program. The meetings took place in the home of the committee chair.

Arriving at the designated time, I marveled at the neighborhood's beauty. The houses were all huge two-story monuments to a South that no longer existed. Sequestered away from the downtown area, the streets were lined with oaks that dripped their moss down over the sidewalks. Along the sidewalks well-dressed couples could be seen holding hands as they strolled before dusk. I entered the home and was told to sit in the living room until the committee was ready for me. I could hear them finishing up with the applicant before me. She was from the Ronald McDonald House and was asking for continuation of last year's grant. Indignation rose within me as I wondered why the McDonald Corporation did not fund that entire operation. After all, the entire world seems to revolve around McDonald's.

When it was my turn, I was ushered into the dining room and took my seat next to ten women each with a mountain of materials spread before her. After asking if I wanted any tea or coffee and making some comments about how nice it was for me to come, they began the review. The lady at the head of the table pulled out a folder of recent newspaper clippings dealing with the shelter. Most of the shelter's recent press dealt with overcrowding and the fact that a murder had taken the life of a former shelter guest. The majority of the interview did not concentrate on the proposal, but on questions of safety. It appeared their stereotypes were also intact. I tried to tell them the shelter was about as safe as any place these days. Crime, after all, occurs everywhere. When the designated sixty minutes were up, I was dismissed even though the conversation was still intense. As I drove home, I wondered if we had already been scratched off their list.

A few days later I received word that we had made the second cut. The next session would be held at a neutral meeting site where the four finalists would be presented to the entire membership. Questions would be prepared in advance and given to us upon arrival. No comments could be made that did not directly relate to the questions. The League did not want to take a chance at being swayed by a passionate plea by one of the applicants. There is no way to prepare for such a presentation, so I marked the day on the calendar and waited.

That night I met the other finalists, including the lady from the Ronald McDonald House. Before the session began, we wished one another luck. I told them I had never been through such a process before and suggested that we form a support group. No one laughed.

Sitting on the stage in front of two hundred members of the Junior League can be intimidating for a male. All I saw was a mass of tailored women who had used gallons of hair spray and tons of make up. When they collectively smiled, the glare was blinding. I had no idea how an appeal to help the homeless would go over with them. To my surprise, most of the questions turned out to be perceptive and of substance. This group had done their homework and now sought to go beyond the superficial understanding that written proposals often leave. I enjoy responding to questions of substance.

Several days later, we received word that we had won. Since that time, the $50,000 has been spent and the volunteer hours exhausted. In two short years, the Magdalene Project moved from an idea to a two-story facility that houses nine family rooms, a women's dormitory for sixteen, and education and office space. Three staff persons operate the facility and many volunteers provide budget workshops, literacy training, after-school care, parenting workshops, and other programs. Members of the Junior League coordinate and operate many of these. If the process proved to be more than met the eye, so did the commitment of the women. What was ultimately accomplished was not so much the building of another shelter, but a monument that signified that two entirely different kinds of women can reach across the social barriers separating them, embrace, and change a small corner of the world.

I also discovered that my own stereotypes were mistaken. Many of the women did, indeed, take off their white gloves to put on work gloves. More than that, however, when they made the commitment to help the homeless, they pushed us to do our part in a better and more organized way than we would have on our own. Just as the shelter challenged and stretched them, the Junior League did the same for us. In the end, both are better off because of the relationship.

> *But above all, my brothers and sisters, do not swear, either by heaven or by earth or with any other oath, but let your yes be yes and your no be no. . . . If any one among you wanders from the truth and someone brings him or her back, let them know that whoever brings back a sinner from the error of his or her way will save their soul and will cover a multitude of sins.*
>
> —James 5:12, 19–20

O God who sees into the heart of each of us,
help me to go beyond the superficial understanding
I often cling to.
Send people to challenge my stereotypes,
confront my prejudice,
and demand I see them for who they really are
and not just how I want to see them.
It is often too easy for me
to place people into categories
instead of seeing them as companions
in the struggle for understanding
and the pursuit of truth.
Help me to break down the classifications I use
so that all are seen as sisters and brothers
who can teach me
just as much as I can teach them.
Help me to refrain from shallow desires
to want people only for what I can get out of them.
Teach me, O God, that commitment goes with charity,
because when one is without the other
all that is left is half-hearted compassion.

— 9 —

Underdressed with Someplace to Go

SHE CALLED, inviting me to a Founders banquet at a private dinner club. At this annual event, a nonprofit agency receives some of the proceeds as a donation for its work. Further, someone from the agency is invited to attend to meet the membership, participate in the banquet, briefly state how the money will be used, and formally receive the contribution. Could I attend? I told her that I would be honored.

A few days later, the official invitation arrived. It informed me of the time and place, who the host would be, and that cocktails would be served. It was printed on a very elegant card. What caught my attention, however, was the bottom right corner. It announced that this would be a "black tie" affair. As the director of a homeless shelter, I have never had reason to purchase a tuxedo; the only time I wore one was at my high school graduation dance. All the weddings I have participated in I have done so as the minister, so I did not wear a tuxedo then either.

I called the club's office to ask if a black tie did indeed mean a tuxedo. She told me that it did. I walked back to the shelter clothing closet to see if one was there. Unusual items of clothing are often donated to the homeless, mostly suits and women's clothes, but you never know. Once someone gave a pair of deep sea diving flippers; at the time I thought someone was telling me in a subtle way that I was in over my head and might need them to keep my nose above water. A quick check, however, showed that no one had contributed a tuxedo to the shelter.

Making some phone calls to board members and volunteers who might know, I inquired about the types of people who would be at the club's Founders dinner. I was told that these were the up-and-coming movers and shakers in the city. They were established names, recognized from the billboards and television commercials advertising their businesses and the many times they have been mentioned in the newspaper. This information proved to be somewhat intimidating.

I calling the club's office back and told the woman in charge I did not have a tuxedo. Further, I explained that as the director I did not feel good about renting one.

"Could you borrow one?" she asked.

I told her I would try. I called everyone I thought might own a tuxedo that would fit me. As I did, I noticed there were many homeless men, women, and children waiting to see me. They would have to wait, however, and I hoped they would understand that raising money is an important function. Without money, ministries cannot continue. While I was called to minister, what I do is motivate people to contribute. Financing by faith is difficult and time consuming.

The phone calls proved to be of no avail. Those I called either had no tuxedo or, if they did own one, it was not the correct size. Dutifully, I called the club's office back and informed the woman of the results of my efforts. She told me to come in a dark suit.

When the night arrived, dressed in our finest, Janice and I arrived for the dinner and rode the elevator to the second floor. After signing in and meeting the host, we met and talked with many of the founders during the cocktail hour. Since I stood out as the only one not wearing a tuxedo (even the waiters looked better than I), many of my conversations began uncomfortably. I would pick someone out, introduce myself, and feel the founder evaluate my clothing. Then the founder would ask me who I was, what I did, and, in some cases, what I was doing there. I identified with how the homeless must feel when they have a job interview. Most will pick out the best the clothing closet has to offer, usually an old suit, a shirt that might match the suit, a tie that might match the shirt, shoes that are not too scruffy, and, if they are lucky, socks that are not white. It is little wonder that few merit serious consideration during the interview. I wondered if these people were judging me the same way.

The meal was one of the finest I have ever had. It began with hot bread with real butter, followed by a cold seafood salad of shrimp, lobster, and salmon and fresh pineapple to clean the palate. Lamb and potatoes were the main course, followed by a garden salad and baked Alaska and coffee. White wine was served with the seafood salad, red wine with the lamb, and champagne with the dessert. I kept thinking of the spaghetti the shelter had served earlier in the evening. The cook had wished there was more meat for it and I had to tell him the budget did not allow for any more. As much as I wanted to enjoy this meal, I found myself with little appetite.

The dinner conversation was enjoyable. When we were not discussing the symphony or someone's newest sailboat, my table companions expressed a great deal of interest in the homeless. Most expressed alarm at the growing number of homeless children and the fact so many were born and raised in our own county. Many seemed to believe that homeless men have an annual convention in New York, get a big map, and pick some warmer place to travel to. In reality, most homeless spend most of their lives close to where they were born.

After dinner the presentation was made. I was handed one of those huge mock checks by the host and everyone applauded. When I was asked to make a few remarks, I tried to explain how no one had donated a tuxedo to the shelter and what it feels like always to be underdressed.

> *... show no partiality as you hold the faith of our Lord Jesus Christ. For if a man with gold rings and in fine clothing comes into your assembly, and a poor man in shabby clothing also comes in, and you pay attention to the one who wears fine clothing ... while you say to the poor man, "Stand there," or "Sit at my feet," have you not made distinctions among yourselves, and become judges with evil thoughts? ... You have dishonored the poor man.*
>
> —James 2:1ff.

God of the underdressed and the naked,
who sees the heart and not the clothes,
why is it we become so preoccupied
with what we wear and how we look?
Why is there more emphasis in this world
on clothing than on compassion?
Why do we dress our charity in fine garments
and make much ado about our giving?
Why must the ministry you call us to
be forced to rely on the whims of the wealthy?
We are preachers who panhandle
with nothing to offer in return
but the opportunity to give.
Did Jesus have to ask for money
as he traveled with the Good News of the Gospel?
I know St. Paul was reduced to asking for money.
How did he feel?
Why is it, Lord, that I am the one who feels funny
when I enter into the midst of those
to whom much has been given?
Is it because you are not with them?
Or are you simply harder to find there?

— 10 —

One Neighbor at a Time

WHEN IT WAS DECIDED that there was a need for a shelter for homeless persons who have AIDS, there was a great deal of discussion about where to locate it. Finding sites for new shelters is very difficult since many people are vocal about not wanting the wrong element in their neighborhoods. Sometimes, however, God provides without much prodding. I shared with a friend that we were looking for a place to serve the homeless HIV population.

"How much can you afford?"

"Nothing," I replied.

She nodded her head and looked as if she felt sorry for me.

"Do you know of anything?" I asked anyway.

She thought for a while before she answered. "You know, before the Catholic Worker House closed, they lived in their house for nothing. Maybe you can try it out."

"Who owns it?"

She told me and I excitedly called Stephen, who was helping with the effort. He wanted to ride over and look at the house immediately. I picked him up, and as we rode over, I told him what I remembered of the house. It was located in a lower middle-class community, mostly black, not far from the downtown area. It was a corner lot with a huge yard. Railroad tracks ran behind it.

It had been built as a Jehovah Witnesses church. It later became a doctor's office, and then the Catholic Worker movement occupied it for several years.

When we arrived, it was apparent the house had been empty for a while. Trash, empty bottles and cans, and needles were strewn throughout the yard. Broken glass lay underneath the windows. The house was dark when we entered the unlocked door. As we tried to catch a vision of what could be, we were suddenly interrupted by noise from another room. Thinking the newest occupants must be crack users, we hurried out and returned to the shelter with just enough vision to continue.

The first thing to do was track down the owner, who now lived in Florida. When he answered the phone, I introduced myself and told him I was interested in his property. He quizzed me about the shelter, who served on the board of directors, and what we intended to do with the property. He told me he would call me right back. Half an hour later he called back.

"Do you want to buy it?" he asked.

"I'd like the same type arrangement you had with the Catholic Worker House," I replied.

"Free?" he exclaimed.

I explained we were a nonprofit agency established to minister to the homeless and seeking to respond to the needs of people with AIDS. We had several such conversations over the following days. He had to check on the taxes, the property value, and several other things. I began to feel we were going to get the house. A few weeks after I first called him, we signed a ten-year lease for one dollar a year.

The next problem was to obtain the funds to renovate the building. One of the members of the board told us of a local foundation that might help. We applied and received an award of $30,000. One of the members of the foundation heard our presentation, looked at the house, and then looked at us. He told us to make it nice. Then he said not to worry about money. This was the first time in my life someone told me that. I began to feel how special, some would say blessed, our efforts were.

With money already in hand, the rehabilitation of the house would take only a couple of months. Before starting, however, we wanted to invite our new neighbors over, tell them about what we were planning, and ask them to participate. As our city has rather strict zoning requirements, obtaining the proper certificates was going to take a while anyway, and this time could be used to meet out neighbors.

On a cold February night, the former crack house hosted members of the board of directors, staff, former residents of the Catholic Worker House, and several dozen neighbors from the community. A brief presentation was made outlining what our intentions were and how we hoped to be an asset to the community. Most listened in silence to what we had to say. When questions were invited, a rotund gentleman who had stood in the doorway throughout the evening said that he wanted to ask us something.

"Are people with AIDS going to stay here?"

"This place is for homeless people who are sick," I replied, "and many of the homeless do have AIDS. So, yes, people with AIDS will be staying here."

The crowd began to murmur as the man continued. "Look, this is a poor, black community. There's a lot of drug abuse around here. Right across the street is called the Shoot Out Corral because so many do their things there. We've already got AIDS here. We don't need any more."

The crowd voiced their approval. Several of us told them how we obtained the property and talked of the great need. We told them how people had no place to go if they were homeless and had AIDS. The hospitals would not keep them. The shelters could not handle them. This place was needed here.

"We don't doubt the need," he replied. "We just don't like it being here."

Frustrated, I told him nothing required us to ask their permission. We wanted to be good neighbors, however, and were inviting their participation. When I said this, the crowd reacted negatively. The man threw his hands up, nodded his head, and told the crowd how we were acting paternalistically.

"Listen," he said, "what we want to know is how come every time a new place is needed for someone, a black community is always chosen? Why don't you try to open where the white folks live?"

He had a point. I could not think of any places for the homeless in mostly white communities. Those communities are typically well organized and powerful. The homeless are kept away from them.

John, the president of the board stood up to speak. "You've got a point. I want you to know that we are Christians. I am a banker, but I'm on this board because I am a Christian and I believe the Bible tells me I'm supposed to take care of people. We found this house first and then we came to you. Maybe we should have come to you first. If we have offended you, we're sorry. We want to be good neighbors and we want your blessings."

The crowd did not respond. The man in the door nodded his head. It appeared as though the apology was what they needed to hear.

"Okay," he said, still standing in the doorway, "but next time you go to open one of these places, try to do it in a white neighborhood first."

We told him we would. A few days later, the permits were granted, and the renovations began. On the day of the grand opening, our new neighbors could be seen cleaning up their yards. The television people came and filmed the event. Members of the community were interviewed and said how much they welcomed us.

A few weeks later, Stephen, now the director of Phoenix Place, was sitting in his office when there was a knock on the door. It was the gentleman from the community meeting. Stephen invited him to sit down.

"Listen," the man began, "I've been watching you ever since

that meeting. You did a good job on this place. It doesn't look like a shelter and it looks good. That helps the neighborhood. I've seen how you take care of these people. I've talked to them, and I think they're good neighbors. They keep the place clean. They speak to me when I walk by. They even invite me in. That's good.

"The reason I'm here," he continued, "is that I was wrong. I thought you were going to use our neighborhood. That's what usually happens. After a place opens up, we don't hear nothing else from them. But you've done a good job. You've worked hard to be a neighbor. I want to be your neighbor too."

When Stephen told me of this meeting, I reminded him of a favorite saying from the Talmud: the world will be saved one neighbor at a time.

> *Now that we have been put right with God through faith, we have peace with God through our Lord Jesus Christ. He has brought us by faith into this experience of God's grace, in which we now live. And so we boast of the hope we have of sharing God's glory! We also boast of our troubles, because we know that trouble produces endurance, endurance brings God's approval, and his approval creates hope. This hope does not disappoint us, for God has poured out his love into our hearts by means of the Holy Spirit, who is God's gift to us.*
>
> —Romans 5:1–5

God who brings people together,
I am always amazed when people
who would not normally be caught dead together
come together.
When understanding and acceptance happens,
it is always a gift.
Most of the time,
we fight hard to be understood.
We fight to be accepted on our terms
when, in fact, it always happens on other terms.
Typically, Lord,

when understanding does come
it is the result of concentrating more
on the job of living up to your word.
Knowing this,
I wonder why I spend so much of my time
trying to convince others of my point of view.
I wonder why it is so important for me
to be accepted for what I say
more than for what I do.
Direct me, Lord,
to the task at hand,
your task,
and you take care of the understanding and affirmation.
I'll be too busy
fulfilling your commandments.

— 11 —

The Breakfast Club

ONE OF THE MISCONCEPTIONS many people have about people who work with the homeless is that we do nothing else. We are stereotyped as wide-eyed radicals who are not homeless ourselves, but barely off the streets. To be sure, there are some who fit this view. There was a time when I fit it, living and working in the inner city, but it proved to be too much for me. The straw that broke the camel's back was a bright Saturday morning that we decided to spend outside as a family. Taking the children to the streets, we were mobbed by other children, starved for attention, wanting to be a part of our family outing. There were too many to say no to. As they trailed along behind us as we walked to the park, the group growing larger with each block we passed, homeless men whom I had worked with all week interrupted us and pulled me to the side to ask me for something more. That night, Janice and I decided that if we were going to continue working with the homeless, we could not live on site. Since then, we have lived elsewhere.

I find no problem with living in a normal American house, but working with the homeless brings a sense of balance to my life that I doubt I would have otherwise. Having the luxury of leaving the crowded shelter and going home makes me thankful for my blessings. When I am behind in my bills and don't know how I can afford braces for my son or glasses for my daughter, I return to the shelter and see the families who slept on the floor the night before and the man who endured the night out. It humbles me and puts my problems in perspective.

I start many of my days by traveling down the road to the "World Famous Breakfast Club" on Tybee Island, Georgia. The Breakfast Club (not to be confused with the movie of the same name) lives up to its name. Owned and operated by Chicago refugees, this breakfast-only restaurant caters to both tourist and locals. It is small and charming, serves great food, and over-whelms visitors with the owners' love of the Cubs and the Bears. Early morning is the gathering time of a group of more or less regular customers. Sitting at the bar instead of in a booth, we dis-cuss over cups of hot coffee anything of interest. While Jody and Bruce cook and the waitresses take a break on a stool beside us, the conversation goes from the sublime to the ridiculous. It is a good way to start the day. While the food is always good, it is the atmosphere and the friends who make the place special and what keeps me returning. It is a meal as it should be, slowly eaten, with friends, in a comfortable setting.

Last year I coached the Breakfast Club Little League baseball team, named the Cubs of course, which is a great way to forget the problems plaguing the world. Nothing is more relaxing than teaching ten-year-olds the fundamentals of baseball, more exhil-arating than leading them to victory, and more frustrating than watching your team lose a game they should have won. During the season, how the team was doing, and we were not doing well, was a regular topic of morning conversation.

The Breakfast Club gathering has become important to me because it is a place where I can go without being stereotyped as a minister to the homeless. Most are aware of what I do, but it just doesn't seem as important as how many fish Bruce caught or how the tourist season is going. This is fine with me, because it means I am not obligated to argue what the church should be doing or explain why the homeless population now includes women and children.

On occasion, however, I find that the world needs a "minister at large." Sliding onto a stool at the Breakfast Club one morning, I ordered my coffee and found myself next to someone I knew as a regular, but not well. We exchanged greetings and listened to a raging debate over how much trash is left on the beach.

"How are things with the homeless?" he asked.

"Business is always too good," I answered.

"I've seen you around and I've heard you're a minister. Is that true?"

I told him I was, as Val refilled my coffee cup.

"You don't look like a minister," he observed.

"What's a minister supposed to look like?" I asked.

"Not like you."

It was true, I guess, although I told him ministers come in all shapes, sizes, colors, and dress. He told me it's harder to pick us out of a crowd than it used to be.

Breakfast was served and we paused to salt and pepper our omelets. The other conversation had escalated to who held the record for finding empty beer cans in their yard.

"Do you ever have people who have to do restitution work at your shelter?" he asked after taking his first bite.

"Sometimes," I responded, "but not very often."

"My daughter got into a little trouble and has to do twenty-five hours of community service," he continued, "and I don't want her going anywhere. Could she do it with you?"

"Sure, but why with me?"

"I love my kids," he explained. "Maybe I overlove them. I try to give them more than I ever had. I might give them too much. I gave her a new car for her birthday. She'll be starting college in the fall, and she got caught drinking and driving. It wasn't much, but she has to do this community service."

Motioning Lori for more coffee, I continued to give him my attention.

"Before she goes off to school, I think it would do her good to see where she could end up if she's not careful. She needs to see the poor up front and close. She doesn't know anything about them right now."

"What exactly do you want her to see?" I asked him.

"How bad life can be if you're not careful," he immediately answered. "I want her to know how lucky she is and what it's like to have to live when you're out of luck."

He grew silent and I finished my breakfast. He ate slowly, as if he were not enjoying his food.

"One more thing," he said as I pushed my plate away. "Can we keep this between us?"

I told him we could and that this kind of thing happens all the time. Very often people ask me to help in situations like this because they are afraid that if they go to another minister, their situation might end up as an illustration in Sunday's sermon. He seemed surprised when I said this.

"You do this all the time?"

"Most of the restitution done at the shelter is performed by people just like your daughter," I explained.

"I thought it would be homeless people who did it."

"That's not true," I said. "Most of the homeless folks I know stay out of trouble and don't have to perform restitution. Several times a year, though, I'll get someone like your daughter. It's rare to have a homeless person doing it."

Standing and grabbing his check, he placed his hand on my shoulder and asked, "Will she be all right down there?"

I told him I would look after her. He thanked me and told me she would be giving me a call. I turned back to my coffee cup. The topic of conversation now centered on how high empty beer cans can be stacked.

You are the light of the world. A city built on a hill cannot be hid. No one lights a lamp and puts it under a bowl; instead he puts it on the lampstand, where it gives light for everyone in the house. In the

same way your light must shine before people, so that they will see
the good things you do and praise your Father in heaven.

—Matthew 5:14–16

God of light in a dark world,
thank you for giving me the time and the opportunity
to get away from the needs when I have to
and be reminded of them when I need to be.
Thank you for places to retreat to
and the chance for my life to strike a balance
between the gifts I have
and the gifts I need to give.
Thank you for turning my light on
when I forget.
Thank you for the position I am in,
which allows me to give to others.
Thank you for the needs of the world,
which offer me a constant reminder
that I am charged to give.
Thank you for the motivation you place in others
to seek me out
when I am not concerned for the needs around me
because I am addressing my own.
Thank you for the struggle I have
to seek a balance in my life
between everything I have
and the knowledge that so many of my friends
have so little.
Thank you for continuing to use me
as an instrument to bring balance in the lives of others.

— 12 —

Answers We Already Know
(Luke 10:20–28)

IT HAPPENED IN A BAR OF ALL PLACES. As we waited for a table in the restaurant, the waitress huddled us into the bar. We were at a seafood place off Highway 80 on Tybee Island. It is located on a turn so sharp that, if you happen to miss it, you might experience the ocean first hand. If you make the turn, though, you will be treated to some of the finest seafood ever.

Usually on trips home, I am treated as something of an oddity. Friends of my parents will call and invite them out. My mother tells them how they would love to come, but her son is visiting. She then asks if Janice and I can come along.

"What does your son do?" they will ask, trying to get some gauge on how I might fit in.

"He's a minister," my mother tells them.

This is usually followed by a brief period of silence, then an exclamation that should not be printed.

At the restaurant, people had a difficult time accepting that I am a minister. There was a visual block. Once we settled down at the table and the food had been ordered, there was a moment or two of forced conversation.

"So, you're a minister?"

"Yes," I answer, "I am." Silence.

My parents try to bail me out. "He runs a shelter and does all kinds of crazy things. He works with the homeless."

The friends try to appear interested as they flag down the waitress for another drink.

These are usually ordeals for me. Because I am stereotyped as a minister, many feel they cannot carry on a normal conversation with me. Whenever the conversation turns to an area I am interested in, politics or some social issue, my comments are accepted with a stare, conveying horror, and the unasked question, "Is this person for real?" The only reason I continue to go to such gatherings is that my parents really do want me to meet their friends.

On this occasion I found myself seated next to a very successful twenty-eight-year-old insurance underwriter whom I had met once before. I knew from conversation that he made a great deal of money. (I am always struck by how so many people measure success by how much money one makes.) He spends most of his weekdays working and most weekends sailing on one of his three sailboats. He loves to race and is quite good at it. Hugh is a very likable fellow. I found myself enjoying his company. While I do not really believe he is a racist, he continually contributes to the cause of racism by using the word "nigger."

When someone uses words like this in my presence, I usually cringe. Rarely, however, do I do anything more. I let my face and my eyes carry some message of disapproval. In my heart of hearts, however, I want to do more. I want to say something really witty that will cut like a knife, letting the person know in no uncertain terms that he or she is going straight to hell. No such comment ever comes to mind.

Next to Hugh, I found myself hoping he would not use *that* word. I did not want to have to come face to face with a glaring example of the dividing wall of hostility. I tried to steer the conversation by asking him what happened at work that day.

"Well, I had to go to this house down town. This nig . . . " and he stopped and looked at me.

My eyes met his and we held one another in tow for a moment. Two very different people froze in some attempt to see inside the other and, perhaps, understand.

"I mean," he began again, "this black fellow . . . " and he went on to relate some insignificant experience.

I thought to myself: Could my mere presence have made some difference? Was it that I had taken some time to get to know Hugh and, once before, had expressed my feeling to him regarding the importance of staying away from terms that keep people apart? Could all the times I cringed have conveyed some feeble message? Had Christ somehow been lifted up in my reluctance to be a prophet?

These are questions that we all face as we try to live a good life. Most people are, deep down, good. They mind their own business and rarely, if ever, get into any kind of trouble. They offer help when they encounter a need. They give something to charity.

This was certainly Hugh's life. He is not a bad person. To the contrary, he does many good things.

He works hard and plays hard and looks just like the average American "yuppie." He is conservative when it comes to business, politics, and just about any other topic he speaks on. Most of the money he makes, he spends on himself. Still, he donates to the United Way and singlehandedly managed to keep his family together through ordeals too lengthy to mention here. While he claims to believe in God, he rarely attends church. All in all, he is a good person. Which brings up a point.

Jesus was once asked what one has to do to inherit eternal life. Jesus responded by asking what the man thought and the man said to love God and neighbor. Jesus told the man he is correct. This leads, of course, to Jesus' parable of the Good Samaritan. Countless sermons have been preached on it, but often the introduction is skipped over.

Tradition has it that the man who asked Jesus the question

was a lawyer. He was obviously accustomed to asking questions, for when Jesus pointed out that the man already knew the answer, the man immediately moved to another question. Lawyers are famous for asking only those questions they already know the answer to.

Of course, lawyers in Jesus' day were different from lawyers today. What do lawyers do? They interpret the law. What was the law back then? It was Roman law because the Romans ruled the country and set the law. The Jewish people, however, claimed that the law of God was the only set of rules they lived by. Lawyers also had to be theologians. This man knew both law and religion.

The problem was that even though he knew his Scripture and could deliver the right answers, he did not have the slightest notion how to apply theology to his life. Things were fine as long as he could define his neighbor in the way he liked. It was another matter, however, when Jesus pointed out that neighbors are more than those who agree with us politically, economically, theologically, or any other way.

Too often proper relationships are sacrificed to a proper theology. Perhaps we have allowed proper theology to subvert proper relationships. While a theology may be correct, our faith is corrupt with indifference and arrogance. We sing how Jesus died for us and how anyone who will just believe may be saved, but we defy the resurrection as something we cannot understand and something too difficult to practice. While we try to live good lives, we do so by keeping our distance from those different from us. Still, we often recognize that regardless of how well we try to live, something is missing in our lives. The question then springs forth: What must I do to inherit eternal life? Certainly we do not dwell on the question much anymore; but it is there, creeping out from time to time.

But, like the lawyer, we already know the answer. In an effort to live with the theology, or lack of theology, that we have carved out, we emphasize particular types of people as neighbors, but functionally leave out many. The people we allow to be our friends usually believe just what we do. Jesus will always challenge this lifestyle.

Once I was speaking at a missions conference in Mississippi. Nathan Porter, a friend who tries to lead churches to care for the poor, was also a speaker. On this day he spoke immediately after I did. We both cited all the Scripture that calls Christians to love people who are different from us. As the invitation was given, a woman asked if she could speak to us.

"I hear what you're saying," she told us as she cried, "but I just can't love black people. I just can't."

I did not know how to respond. Her tears were overwhelming me, but Nathan took charge. "This is great," he said. "You have come forward to admit to God that you recognize your ignorance and prejudice. Let us thank God that you are admitting how stupid it is to live a Christian life while holding onto these things."

Making us all hold hands, Nathan led us in prayer. As he finished, he told the woman that recognizing the problem is half of the solution. Now that she knows she is prejudiced, she can ask for forgiveness and seek to become "un-prejudiced."

"What I want you to do," he told her, "is to leave this conference now and find some ministry with black children. After a while you'll learn to love them. Then go see your preacher and tell him what you have done."

Bewildered, the lady nodded and left. Nathan told me it had been a great day.

"Love the Lord your God with all your heart and with all your soul and with all your mind" and "Love your neighbor as you love yourself." The first permits the second and the second reveals the first. Because we love God, we seek to make all people our neighbors, not just the ones who happen to make us comfortable. Because we love our neighbor, we see the presence of God in the world. This is the road to eternal life.

Too often, we allow our theology to sweep us into causes. We fight for the things our theology teaches and seek to save the entire world at once. We forget, however, that Jesus saved the world one person at a time.

Hugh has become my friend, although we are not much alike. We have little in common. Still he is my neighbor, and I want to get to know him better. Looking around, I see so many others I don't know yet. I trust I am open enough to introduce myself and hear what they have to say to me. Perhaps, too, they might hear what I have to say to them.

PART THREE

Partners in Love

IF LOVE IS WHAT MAKES THE WORLD GO ROUND, it is a wonder this globe turns at all. Many claim they desire love more than anything else. But in the end many will opt to keep money, security, status, or respect before love.

St. Paul says that love is God's greatest gift to us. St. John claims that God is love, so the greatest gift from God is God. This is hard to believe because we do not necessarily get God in the way we want. What we get is God the way God actually is. Such honesty is too much for many to handle.

While the actual gift may confuse us, the principle should not. Such principles always do seem to confound, however, because they offer no guarantee. The only way to receive love is to give it away. The more love we give away, the more we receive. Knowing that God gave everything away when we got Jesus, it is hard not to wonder what God got in return.

— 13 —

The Father of the Homeless

Most of the families who come to the shelter have a single parent — typically, the mother. This one was no exception. She brought her two sons and moved onto the overflowing space on the dining room floor. From the very beginning, it was obvious that she had special problems. Each day she would disappear for hours, leaving her boys with whomever would agree to watch them. Word soon drifted to the front that she was a "rock star," addicted to crack/cocaine. At five dollars a pop, it is very easy to obtain crack, and it is a cheap and instant high. Pete, one of the social workers who seeks to help substance abusers, told me that everyone wants to feel better and people take drugs to feel better faster.

Tony, age eight, and Robert, age four, never seemed to mind when their mother was gone. They would color pictures, listen to stories, or play in the courtyard until she returned. Then they would hug her tight, stay as close as possible to her, and beg for her to take them to the park. Her attitude grew worse, however, and we began to suspect child abuse.

One day she left and did not return. At first, Tony and Robert did not seem to mind. They were content to color, read, and play.

When night came and she still was not back, the staff began to worry. The next morning, the boys grew anxious and began to cry for their mother. That night we decided that we could wait no longer.

A child abuse caseworker was called to the shelter. We were told Tony and Robert would be placed in a foster home unless another relative could be located. As I was discussing the options with her, Tony tugged at my coat.

"Mr. Elliott," he said with tear-filled eyes, "can we please stay here? We know that momma will be back soon."

I looked to the staff for help. Harriet rushed over and gave the children candy. Dianne questioned them about relatives who might be nearby. Sharon gave them pieces of white paper and crayons so they would think of something else. I returned to studying the options that were available to them.

The police arrived, since they are called in any case of abandonment. As I walked to greet them, I passed by Tony and Robert sitting on the floor concentrating on their coloring. I noticed that both had drawn houses with families standing in front — a father, mother, and two boys. I was struck that even homeless children dream the American dream.

Dianne noticed it too. "I see that you have a father in your picture. Do you know where your father is?"

Tony looked up. "He lives around here somewhere."

We all stopped and looked at Tony. "Do you know where?" several asked at the same time. Tony said that he did not.

"Do you know his name?" Dianne asked.

Tony told us that he did. A quick check of the phone book showed that such a name indeed existed. Dianne hurried to her office to call the number.

A half hour later, a tall man still dressed in work clothes rushed through the door. Both boys greeted him at the same time. They rushed to him as the reborn family embraced. After a short celebration, the father asked how we got the kids.

We told him how their mother checked into the shelter several days ago and what had happened since then. Tears filled the large man's eyes.

"They're homeless?" he asked in a deep broken voice. "I didn't know."

"What happened?" we asked.

"Several months ago," he began, "we divorced. She got custody, although I fought for it. I knew that she used drugs. That's why we divorced. After it was over, she just dropped out of sight. I haven't heard from her since. This is the first time I've seen my babies."

He cried again and hugged them tighter and with more joy than I've seen in most families. The police asked several questions and completed their report. The caseworker said that in light of the father's arrival, she would no longer be needed. We helped Tony and Robert gather their few possessions and load them in their father's car. Before he left, he warmly shook my hand.

"I used to think that all homeless people were winos," he said. "I didn't know there were families. I never thought they might be my family."

Then he got in the car and joyfully drove home.

What man among you, if he has a hundred sheep and has lost one of them, does not leave the ninety-nine in the open pasture and go after the one who is lost, until he finds it? And when he has found it, he lays it on his shoulders, rejoicing. And when he comes home, he calls his friends and neighbors, saying to them, "Rejoice with me, for I have found my sheep which was lost!"

—Luke 15:4–6

God of the lost and the little,
I rejoice when some are found!
There are too many in this world
who have no sense of direction,
who listen to the misleading guidance of others,
and who wind up in places

where they really should not go.
Too many adults, Lord,
are too childish to be parents.
They are not responsible,
or their burdens are too much for them to bear.
Thinking of themselves first,
they forget the children
and abuse them through neglect.
Too many children, Lord,
have grown up toc fast.
They must give up their innocence,
never to get it back.
Too many parents, Lord,
never fully know what is happening with their children.
They have lost them somehow
in the difficult maze of living a life
that has too much neglect and too much selfishness.
Yet sometimes, O Lord,
little ones are found!
And the rejoicing in heaven
is little match for the rejoicing
that is felt on earth!

— 14 —

A Prodigal Son's Father

ONE OF THE THINGS I find happening a lot at the shelter is that many of my phone calls are from people trying to understand how homelessness has affected their lives. Many reason that homelessness is something to be seen only on television or passed by on a street corner. For others, homelessness is a charity they can give to when they feel the need. Still others believe the homeless are nothing more than men and women who deserve such a status because they drink, use drugs, or are simply too lazy to hold jobs. When it happens to someone they know or love, however, many seek some deeper understanding of America's most visible social ill.

The phone rang again that morning. My greeting was a weary one.

"Mike, is that you?" came a voice I did not recognize.

"Yes, this is Mike. Can I help you?"

"You don't remember me," she said. "This is Pam Jones."

My mind raced back to my childhood. Her son was one of my old chums. Alan and I had played together and gone to the same schools, but eventually we lost track of one another as we began to build our own lives. Pam, his mother, had been a baby-sitter, Sunday School teacher, and friend of my parents during earlier years. I remembered her as a pretty woman who loved her children and was active in her church. She had lost her husband to cancer several years earlier. I had already moved to another city when he died, but I did send her a card when I found out about it. Mr. Jones had been my baseball coach and had taken me, along with my father, to my first professional league baseball game.

"It's good to talk to you," I said. "How are you?"

She told me she had remarried, had a career, and still lived in the old neighborhood. Then I heard the seriousness take hold of her voice and the conversation took a turn down a dark path. She had stepchildren now. One of them, Jack, had been a problem, got messed up in a bad relationship, and lost his job. She wanted to know if he had stayed at the shelter. After a quick check of the files, I told her that he had. I heard her voice crack out a response and I listened to her cry.

"Pam," I began, "this is not atypical of how people become homeless. When their primary relationships break down, many do not have enough support to maintain their jobs. Once that happens, they can't pay the bills and eventually they lose their homes."

"We think he's into drugs, too," she sobbed.

"That's not unusual, either. People who are in a bad situation want to feel better. Drugs make people feel better. That is why people use them. Unfortunately, they don't stop to consider the ramifications of their actions."

"We began to suspect it when we kept missing money at our home. One night we asked him and he ran out of the house. We haven't seem him since."

"How long ago was that?" I asked.

"Two months."

She went on to ask if I could find the time to have lunch with her and George, her husband. I said I could, and we chose the date and place. That night I tried to find Jack, but he didn't check into the shelter. Several days later, I met with her and George.

George was a large man with a firm grip and rough hands. He

told me he had seen me on the news a lot. We ordered our food and he asked me what he should do.

"About what?" I asked back, not wanting to give them simple answers that would not accomplish much.

"About Jack," he said in a sad voice. "I've got to do something or I'll go crazy."

"I'm afraid there isn't much you can do. It mostly comes down to what Jack wants to do. You could offer him all the help in the world, but if he doesn't want it, it will not do much good."

"But he's my son." George's eyes blinked back tears. He did not look like the kind of man who would cry.

"From the moment our children are born, we begin to prepare them to leave us. When they take their first baby steps, they are taking the first steps away from us — away from the protection we offer and the love we can give. While we still have them at home, hopefully we can convince them they can always come back if they need to."

"But I don't want a prodigal son," he blurted.

"Well, I'm afraid you've got one. Every homeless person is someone's son or daughter or father or mother. In some ways you're lucky. You still have an idea of where Jack is. You know he's still alive. You know he's not going hungry."

"But I want to take care of him." George said forcefully.

"And I pray that someday soon Jack will let you. Right now, though, he has to answer some questions for himself. I hope he will get to the point where he is strong enough to ask for your help. The fact of the matter, however, is that you cannot answer Jack's questions for him. Only he can."

George picked up his fork and played with it. Pam squeezed his arm to let him know she was there. I felt like the bearer of bad news and did not care for the role.

"So," George sighed, "the story of the Prodigal Son just has to play itself out?"

I nodded. "It's a story that happens a hundred times a day at the shelter."

"Do they ever go home again?"

"Sometimes," I softly replied, "and sometimes not."

George looked at Pam and said he needed to get back to the office. They thanked me for coming. Both agreed they would read the parable of the Prodigal Son that evening. George said they would read it every night until Jack came home. I hope they are not having to read it now, but I never heard from them again.

Now many days later, the younger son gathered all he had and took his journey into a far country, and there he squandered his property in loose living.... His father saw him and had compassion....

—Luke 15:11ff.

Every night, I watch them come to the shelter, Lord.
I know that they used to belong to somebody.
Each one is someone's
son or daughter,
brother or sister,
aunt or uncle,
father or mother.
I watch them come from another day spent outside,
looking for work,
or passing the time,
or trying to feel better for a while.
I see them eat what was prepared,
shower and change into donated clothes,
climb into their assigned beds
and restlessly sleep
in preparation for another day
just like the one before.
I wonder about their fathers and mothers
and why they do not rise from their beds
so they can flee home and be taken in.
Are their fathers and mothers waiting for them?
Planning the celebration for homecoming?

— 15 —

Friends Who Know

SITTING OUTSIDE ON A FALL DAY at the St. Martin's Afro-German Tea Room for lunch is one of the most pleasant ways to spend an afternoon. The wonderful restaurant is nestled in the courtyard between the massive Gothic church and the huge rectory. There are barrels full of flowers to view, statues of saints standing nearby, and a magnificent view of the church's stained-glass window. Located in the inner city of Louisville, Kentucky, the restaurant was the brainchild of Father Vernon Robertson. Having a rectory with more room than he would ever need and a congregation abandoning the downtown area, he decided the best way to continue funding the Montessori School would be to use the available space, open a restaurant, staff it with as many volunteers as possible, and give all the profit to the school. He recruited his sister to run the kitchen, the conversion was made, and the St. Martin's Afro-German Tea Room opened. The name always draws a reaction. St. Martin's is the name of the church. It is located in an old German neighborhood that is now mostly black, hence Afro-German. Once finished, the converted rectory looked like a tea room.

I met Father Robertson during a dry period in my spiritual life. The struggles of being pastor to the homeless coupled with

Baptist bureaucracy had left me empty, so I began to visit other churches in the neighborhood instead of going to lunch. I learned that only Catholic churches offer a daily service at noon. One day I wandered into St. Martin's. Lovely organ music was provided for fifteen minutes before each service and continued throughout the Mass. Some thirty people gathered in a sanctuary built to accommodate fifteen hundred. The priest proclaimed a message rooted as much in Barth as the pope and I was hooked. It became an almost daily custom for me, a Southern Baptist minister, to attend a noonday mass.

Soon afterward, I called and invited Father Robertson to lunch. Although approaching sixty, he told me to call him Vernon. He had lost none of the zeal for life that keeps one young. He told me he was liturgically conservative and socially progressive. We immediately fell into a dialogue concerning how the church is to save the world. I argued the world was going to hell and the church needed to move quickly. He said anything we could do would only prove to be a kink in the chain of history.

"Give it another thousand years," he said.

"A thousand years!" I exclaimed. "The Gospel is more urgent than that!"

He also told me that Southern Baptists and Roman Catholics are more alike than any other religious groups. I told him I did not agree and asked how he could say that.

"Infallibility of the pope ... infallibility of the Bible ... it's the same thing," he responded.

Our friendship grew quickly and deeply. Soon, we established our routine. Each Wednesday at noon, I would attend Mass, sometimes participating as the reader. Each Wednesday evening, he would attend our midweek prayer service. Both congregations took notice of our relationship and the churches entered into a covenant to work together in ministering to the community. We dubbed this arrangement "The Roman Catholic/Southern Baptist Coalition." The meetings occurred whenever we had lunch together.

On this fall day, we washed down our servings of Apple Crisp with strong coffee. Our discussion had centered around why God had called us into the ministry and, more specifically, ministry with the poor. We pushed one another past the superficial answers we normally used and looked deeply into our lives for what had shaped us. When was the first time we had recognized the need to respond to poverty? Good friends know when to continue pushing and when to stop. Vernon knew I was struggling to understand my calling and continued to challenge what I said.

Finally I told him I remembered one Christmas. My family had not been wealthy. Like most Americans in the 1960s, my parents lived to fulfill the American Dream. They worked hard, managing to get the right house and just enough income to keep it. The children were excited that Christmas was here. We kept telling our parents what we wanted. Finally Christmas Eve arrived, but there was little under the tree. That afternoon, I saw my father sitting in the front yard, his feet hanging into the ditch that ran along the street, waiting. His paycheck arrived by mail then, although I did not know that this was why he was waiting. As I stared out the window, I saw my mother go sit beside him, her feet also hanging in the ditch. I wondered what they were doing and went outside and took my place next to them. When I asked, they replied they were waiting on the mailman.

Soon afterward, my younger brother noticed us and sat next to me. Later, my sister ceased playing and also sat next to us. We all thought the family was just spending time together in the middle of the day. I did not remember what we talked about, but I can recall the pleasant feeling of being with the people I loved most in the world and knowing they loved me. I am sure we children talked about what Santa Claus would bring us that night.

Finally, the red, white, and blue mail truck appeared at the end of the street. My father jumped to his feet and stood by the mailbox. The rest of the family watched him. Ever so slowly the mail truck inched closer. Eventually, the mail carrier arrived at to our house, handed my father the mail, and wished us a Merry

Christmas. My mother stood beside my father as he sorted the mail. When he finished, his hand dropped and he looked at my mother. She took his arm and offered it a hug. He looked at us with pain in his eyes before he turned and locked arms with my mother and walked to the house.

At that moment it dawned on me that he had been waiting for his check and that it had not come. He needed it for our Christmas. Jumping up, leaving my brother and sister behind, I ran to them. I do not remember if I said anything or even if I hugged them, but I do recall the feeling. It has never left me.

When I finished telling all this to Vernon, he asked me if I was going to cry. I said that I might. We agreed that God began to call me to the ministry on that day.

> *Now the word of the Lord came to me saying, "Before I formed you in the womb I knew you, and before you were born I consecrated you. . . . "*
>
> —Jeremiah 1:5

God who knew me
before I knew there was a God,
I sometimes look at where my life has gone,
second-guessing my decisions,
deciding what I would change
and what I would keep the same.
Thank you for your consistent presence
throughout my days.
Thank you for dear friends
who force me to pause
and consider you
when I am much too preoccupied with myself.
Thank you for those times
when you reached down into my life
and gave me understanding
for the things I did not comprehend.

Thank you for helping me to swallow
whatever it was
that prevented me from jumping to my feet,
running to those who needed to be loved,
and at least trying somehow to respond.
Thank you for the insight
to look back and discover
that you have been with me all along,
knowing me better
than I knew myself.

— 16 —

Living through "Love"

STAFF MEETING is a time when we celebrate that we have survived another week. The atmosphere is typically festive with bouts of seriousness. We all report on the status of our efforts and relate any significant happenings since the last meeting. Recently, a new program had been put into place and its status was being reviewed.

Stephen was responsible for answering calls that came on the AIDS hotline. The shelter had backed into addressing AIDS issues after it was discovered that 10 to 20 percent of the guests were HIV positive. One had nearly died in the shelter and this served as motivation to respond to these needs. A facility, Phoenix Place, was opened for homeless persons who have AIDS and the hotline was put in place to answer questions people have concerning the disease.

At eight o'clock the phone rang. Stephen answered and heard a young man's voice.

"How do you catch AIDS?" he nervously asked.

Stephen was always amazed at how ignorant most are concerning the illness. Briefly, he ran through the canned speech and told the caller that AIDS cannot be caught except through sexual contact or common use of a needle when using drugs. AIDS is not passed through casual contact, hugging, drinking from the same glass, or using the same toilet seat. In fact, of all the contagious diseases, AIDS is the least contagious.

As he spoke, Stephen recalled how the board of directors had reacted when they learned he had AIDS. At the time, he was the shelter cook. The board meetings were at noon and lunch was normally served. Reacting with fear, the board scheduled a meeting at the dining room in a hospital where one of them worked to deal with the issue. Most argued they wanted nothing to do with AIDS, but were told, for better or worse, it was in the shelter to stay. Most of the concern centered on the fact that someone with AIDS worked in the kitchen. Finally, the hospital administrator said the food that had just been consumed had probably been prepared by someone with AIDS. He told them they simply could not catch it that way. Ultimately a vote was taken, Stephen was allowed to stay, and the new programs for the HIV positive population were initiated. When the board met at the shelter again, however, not many ate the lunch prepared for them.

"Well," the young man interrupted Stephen's speech, "if I wear a condom, I won't catch it, will I?"

Stephen quickly reviewed the precautions. Non-oxynal-9 should be used with the condom for the best protection. The caller thanked Stephen and hung up.

A few hours later, the same young man again called the hotline. "Will you explain about the condom and that other stuff again."

Stephen again explained the process.

"Does the jelly stuff go inside or do you rub it on the outside?"

Stephen explained how it went and the caller hung up. A short time later the same caller rang again.

"Can you use it twice?"

"What?" asked Stephen.

"The condom...can you use it twice?"

Stephen explained he could not.

"I have to get another one?"

"If you are going to practice safe sex, " Stephen said patiently, "you have to."

When Stephen recounted this story in staff meeting the following Monday, everyone laughed at the caller's ignorance before an uneasiness filled the room. Phoenix Place had only been open a few weeks and it was already full. A waiting list had started and it was getting longer. While no one had attacked our ministry to people with AIDS, we expected such attacks. Comments had already been made about how people who get AIDS deserve it.

Some of the guests at Phoenix Place were growing sicker by the day. Death loomed in the air. Sitting around the table that morning, we all knew there was another young man out there somewhere who, through ignorance, was in the process of becoming the latest casualty of AIDS. Everyone also knew Phoenix Place was full.

The young man's search for love had touched a deep cord within everyone. He wanted immediate satisfaction with token thought given to possible ramifications. He was willing to risk his life for a fleeting moment of pleasure. We all hoped he lived through it.

Many waters cannot quench love, neither can floods drown it. If a man offered for love all the wealth of his house, it will be utterly scorned.

— Song of Solomon 8:7

For I have an obligation to all peoples, to the civilized and to the savage, to the educated and to the ignorant. So then, I am eager to preach the Good News to you also....

— Romans 1:14–15

God who is true love,
I live in the midst of utter confusion.
I find that I do not recognize love when I see it,
and that I often confuse other things for it.

I have read the discourses on love in your word,
but still I am ignorant.
And I live in a world full of ignorance.
I am one of many
who define love by what we see on television
or read in drugstore romances.
These seem to convey so much more...
passion?
I know of too many
who chased after what they thought was love
only to find it was something else.
Their relationships grow sick
and every day they die a little.
Then today there are those
who grab at love
only to find death.
These are judged harshly be their peers.
But what have they done that is so wrong?
They looked for love,
but settled for less.
And while I try to live a life motivated by love,
I sometimes wonder
what I'm settling for.

— 17 —

Rediscovering Love

BEFORE HE RETIRED FROM THE MINISTRY, Robert had been a powerful voice of compassion and dignity in the city. His congregation was old, large, and rich. Many of the city's "movers and shakers" were part of his flock. Because of this, he had been powerful. His opinion had been sought by many, his presence was coveted at important meetings, and his participation was much needed by anyone wanting to do anything in the community. His name meant something to most who heard it and his reputation could go no higher. He was a force in the city and, recognizing his power, he tried to make a difference. But this was before he retired.

His father had died early, having worked himself to the grave. Robert had promised himself to quit early enough to have time in his later days. He wanted to read all the books that had stacked up over the year, to travel when he wanted and not to have to "be there" whenever anyone needed him. He wanted some life just for himself. So he kept the promise and retired.

Everyone reacted with sad surprise when he made the announcement. During his final service as leader, gifts were given, accomplishments were cited, and tearful farewells were bestowed upon him. Many commented on how missed he would be, and

Robert replied he was not going anywhere, just retiring. It was a day for remembering the past, however, so he gave little thought to the future. He had not really changed, he thought to himself. He was still the powerful person he had been before he retired, or so he thought.

The first few months of retirement were happy ones. He read, took walks, and mostly did whatever his wife wanted to do. They traveled oversees and looked up old friends. He tried to write and discovered he was not a writer. Church became difficult for him when he discovered it is easier to be a leader than a follower. What bothered him most, however, was the power that slipped away. At meetings he found his opinions did not mean as much as before. His presence was not required any longer. Most seemed surprised he bothered to come at all. All this led to a depression that quickly deepened and ruined his later years. His wife noticed and challenged him to get involved with something, but he was not used to having to work at fitting in.

He eventually gave up and decided to stay at home. He ceased reading, concentrating instead on mindless television. Everything his wife suggested was a bad idea. He lost his energy and quit taking walks. Life became something to bear, more than something to use. He felt used and discarded by the people he had tried to give so much to. He resented them for it.

Two things pulled him out of it. First, he attended a community consensus seminar based on M. Scott Peck's *The Different Drum*. Here he shared his feeling and, for the first time, he felt others heard him. Throwing himself into the building of community, he made himself available to anyone who wanted to try. He now felt community was more important than power, and he tried to convince anyone who would stop long enough to listen.

He also discovered the homeless. Always interested in social issues, he had been aware of their plight, but at the invitation of a friend he attended a meeting of shelter workers and was drawn into the world of the poor. He began to attend their meetings and volunteer for their functions. He learned how little affirmation people who work with the homeless receive. With his ideas of consensus, he forced people who competed for the same funds to work together. He made them listen to one another rather than endure endless speeches. Most importantly, he took the time to ask how individuals were doing. He would call or stop by the shelters and visit with whomever was there, always offering words of encouragement and affirmation. He became a minister to a group of ministers who had no minister.

His life snapped back into place. His wife noticed his new purpose. Once he managed, only because of everyone's appreciation of him, to get all the ministers to the homeless to spend a precious Saturday together discussing the need for community in the homeless world. At first, everyone had defenses up, but as Robert quietly pleaded, they were lowered. He spoke of how the love we have is so directed at only the homeless, we often forget the other love in the world. It needs to be rediscovered, he told us. There is too much pain in life not to have all the love we can possibly get. He told us his story of leaving power, and losing love, only to rediscover love in the last place he expected — in the world of the homeless.

He has brought down mighty kings from their thrones and lifted up the lowly. He has filled the hungry with good things, and sent the rich away empty handed.

—Luke 1:52–53

But when you give a feast, invite the poor, the maimed, the lame, the blind, because they cannot repay you....

—Luke 14:14

If any one would be first, he must be last and servant of all.

—Mark 9:35

God of love,
who often leads me to rediscover love
in places I had forgotten,

hear my commitment
to follow love
wherever it leads.
To follow through valleys
and over dangerous mountain trails;
to follow down dirty city streets
and in the gutters of my town;
to follow down the sidewalks
of manicured lawns
and through the doors of offices
housing the rich and the powerful:
where love leads me,
I will follow.
There are too many times
when I follow only the love
I am comfortable with.
Too often I give only to those
I like in the first place.
Forgive me for loving some
by hating others.
My love is too often misguided.
So you lead, Lord.
I will follow.

— 18 —

Why Love the Poor?
(James 2:5–7)

WHEN I WAS SEVENTEEN YEARS OLD, I found myself at home one evening, alone with my father. We were not close. I thought he went out with the Stone Age and he thought I should be locked in a zoo somewhere. Once, looking at my long hair, he asked when I was moving into a cave with the other prehistoric men.

"As soon as I can figure out how to build one," came my sarcastic response. Most of the conversation we had was not much better.

On this particular night, it was just the two of us. I came out of my room, where I listened to loud music, and walked to the kitchen to get something to eat. At his usual place at the head of the table, my father was reading the paper. After rummaging through the cupboards, I complained with typical hostility that there was never anything to eat.

Instead of getting on me for my attitude problem as he usually did, my father looked at me and suggested we go get something. Together! We had not spent any real time together in a couple of years. We were simply so different. He never seemed to understand anything I wanted and I thought he simply never could.

After a few moments of awkward silence, I asked what he wanted.

"I'd like some crab meat," he replied.

We lived on the coast, so seafood was plentiful and cheap. It sounded good, so we jumped in the car, went to a nearby crab house, ordered two dozen crabs, and drove back home.

At the kitchen table again, we feasted on the white meat and washed it down with beer. There wasn't much dinner conversation. After a while, however, near the end of the crabs, I asked him something. The question had formed a few nights earlier, when he had hosted some of his friends. That night they swapped war stories. All had been in the Korean conflict; the Vietnam War was raging as they spoke. Most of their stories had been humorous ones, as no one seemed willing to discuss the horrors of war. This night I brought the subject up again.

"Tell me about war."

He looked at me for a long time. I recall feeling uncomfortable in the silence. After a long, deep drink from his beer, he spoke in hushed tones.

"I was about your age because I lied to get into the Marines. We were in a town, checking out each house door to door, trying to get anyone still there to leave. We were bombing the city and, while the bombing had ceased for a while, it would be starting up again.

"At one place the windows had been blown out, and we were cautious. Like most of the houses, this one was in shambles. Kicking the door open, we found ourselves face to face with an old man sitting in the middle of a large room. Broken chairs and papers littered the place. It was dark, so it took a few moments for our eyes to adjust. We began to tell him he would have to leave, that the fighting wasn't over, and that he was still in danger.

"We saw he was not listening, but was trying to tell us something. Then we saw he had no legs. They had been blown off by a bomb and had maggots crawling over the bloody stubs. Holding a stick, crying as he tried to explain something to us, he wiped his legs with the stick. We tried to understand but couldn't. Finally, as he pointed to his legs and then to our rifles, we understood. He wanted us to shoot him. We froze."

My father grew silent. His eyes were moist. I had never seen him cry before and only would on two other occasions — standing before his mother's grave and at my wedding. He took another long drink from his beer.

"What did you do?" I asked.

Looking at me again, he spoke even slower. "We were just kids. We debated a long time because we had never shot anyone before. Hell, we had hardly fired our guns. None of us wanted to be there. The old man kept crying and wiping the maggots from where his legs were supposed to be. It seemed as if all time had stopped. Finally, we agreed we would point our guns, close our eyes and count to three. Then whoever wanted could pull the trigger. No one had to shoot. We aimed. I closed my eyes tighter than I ever had. We counted in unison. One . . . two . . . three. . . ."

He grew silent again. Staring at him, his eyes were red and wet, I asked, "What did you do?"

He looked past me, but didn't speak. In that moment, I felt closer to him than I ever had or have been since. I wanted to hug him and tell him that I love him, but our distance prevented me from doing so. I sat and waited for an answer, all the time visualizing the old man wiping where his legs should have been. My father clutched his empty beer can tightly, stood up, and walked out the door. I heard the car engine start and he pulled out of the driveway. He has never answered my question.

"Blessed are the peacemakers; for they shall be called children of God." The problem, of course, is that few of us know much about waging peace, but we have perfected the art of waging war. Just when the world seems to settle down into absence of conflict, another fight breaks out and the winds of war blow hard, silencing any call to peace.

Perhaps the reason peace cannot be obtained on any grand scale is because few of us are really at peace with ourselves. Each of us has wars being waged inside. The contradictions that make up our lives are in battle for dominance. Even the meekest individual is a walking contradiction, well meaning at heart, but hypocritical in action. We will weep tears over the child on the nightly news in need of a transplant, but accept without a pang the death of hundreds of thousands from malnutrition. The loss of an airplane is an epic tragedy; tribal genocide in South Africa is a paragraph hastily read and quickly forgotten. We pledge money to rock stars for hungry people in the Third World, but drive by community soup kitchens with little thought of how they make their budgets. We are good people who do not know how to be good.

Unfortunately, the role of the church means very little to people who are at war with themselves. Once a person came to me who was at war with alcoholism. With a painful lack of understanding, he outlined the problem for many.

"I've come to church and I've asked for help. I invited Jesus into my heart, whatever that means. I try to do good. I pray not to but I still drink. Tell me then what earthly good the church is?"

It brought to mind a statement John McKinsey once made: "The Church will never die. It will only give such a convincing appearance of death that most will be absolutely convinced that she is dead." Indeed, when it comes to peace too, often the church moves as if it has rigor mortis, all too often not doing much earthly good.

Recently I was taping a local television show when I was asked what role the church had played in the recent establishment of a ministry for homeless persons who have AIDS. When I told the interviewer that the church played no role, he seemed surprised and asked me to explain.

"Churches have abdicated the social side of the Gospel. We skip over those sections of the Bible. The fact that the Scriptures spend more time discussing caring for the needy and practicing justice than any other topic means little to most congregations. We would rather search for an individual absence of conflict, some private peace where we ask the Lord to take away our thorns. It has become apparent to the church that it cannot save the world, so it tries to save itself. We have completely forgotten that Jesus said we must lose our lives in order to save them."

He asked me what one Christian was supposed to do.

"All you can do," I replied, "is love your life enough to live it, accept it for what it is, and share it with others."

The gift of life must be accepted, then given away. Once we learn to love life, all life, then we become protective of the lives of others. We become aggressive in our love of their lives even when they have not yet learned to love their own lives. The Scriptures call for us to defend the cause of the poor and the needy, to share what we have with others, always to remember the widows, the orphans, and the sojourners. Jesus went so far as to say the poor will be with us always. Why? So that we will always have someone on whom to target our love and concern. Such attention means that our struggles to live a Christian life are always focused on human need. Our resources are directed outward and, because they are, our internal struggles for peace are addressed. The miracle of the Gospel is that it is only by giving our love away that we learn how to love ourselves. Jesus gave us the poor so that we would always have someone to love.

Unfortunately, churches have diminishing concern for the poor. It is an old problem, however. James warned in his letter about ignoring their needs. (Churches have never liked this, of course, and James's letter barely made it into the Bible!) Throughout the Bible, however, runs a thread calling our attention to the poor. While most choose to ignore these passages, surely God repeated the message so often because we need to be convinced. Knowing how selfish and inward we can be, God reminds us how to look outward instead of inward. In short, if we are going to be Christians at all, we need the poor to do it.

Why should we love the poor? Because God tells us to love them time and time again. If this is not enough reason, and history has proven it is not, then we need to love them for our own sakes. Peace cannot be obtained in our lives without them.

At the shelter I see it happen every day. People volunteer. They find something they are comfortable doing. Along the way, human need becomes personalized for them. They enter into a relationship with a homeless person and try to help. As the relationship continues, however, they make a great discovery. They received more help than they gave! "In fact," claims Leo Buscaglia, "it is usually the helper who is helped through helping!" (*Bus 9 to Paradise,* p. 9).

There are too many who struggle for peace in their lives, only to be frustrated in their efforts. They turn inward, looking to have only their own needs met. The simplicity of God's alternative causes most to miss it. Peace is found through struggle. Love is found by giving love away. Acceptance is discovered by accepting others. Help is found by offering help.

PART FOUR

Partners in Doubt

FREDERICK BUECHNER says that doubt is "the ants in the pants of faith" (*Wishful Thinking*, p. 20). If this is true, it is a wonder I have not been eaten alive. It is so easy to doubt. I doubt my faith in God as well as any faith God might have in me. I doubt that the things I am hoping for are really the things I need to have a happier life. I doubt my wife's love for me and my love for her. I even doubt if my doubts are legitimate doubts!

I have found that as long as I struggle with the questions, God still speaks somehow and I sometimes hear. My hopes sustain me until tomorrow, my wife does indeed love me as I do her, and the doubts are worthwhile enough to continue struggling with. While I may not find many answers, I discover many legitimate questions. Why do good things happen to bad people? Why do the wicked prosper? Why do so many people say all the right things, but never seem to do them? Why is God so silent when I need something to be thundered from the heavens?

While struggling with such questions may not lead to answers, it does leave an interesting conclusion: the answers are simply not as important as the struggle. In my day-to-day life, the bigger picture is insignificant in light of the smaller triumphs.

— 19 —

A Broken Family Tree

RICHARD HAD THREE STRIKES AGAINST HIM. He was homeless and had come to the shelter because almost all his significant relationships had been terminated — by himself or by others. Loud, abusive, and selfish, Richard would demand more than anyone could give him. At church he would often stand up in the midst of worship and cause some sort of disturbance. He would challenge something the minister had said, begin proclaiming his own gospel, or mumble loudly to himself. Only Stephen still called him friend.

He had AIDS, too, and this is what brought him to the shelter. Hospitals recognize that it is not cost-efficient to care for those who have AIDS. It is cheaper to treat them as outpatients and send them on their way. Unfortunately, once Richard was recognized as one of "that kind of people," no one would rent to him or allow him to stay with them. Once his illness was discovered at the shelter, he was moved into the tiny medical clinic. By this time, sores were all over his body, oozing blood and body fluids onto the sheets each night. No one wanted to go near him. Stephen, another homeless resident who had tested HIV positive, volunteered to care for him. Richard's situation caused much fear and confusion in the shelter. Other residents asked me daily what was wrong with the man in the clinic. I didn't want to tell them. Hysteria might break out and homeless shelters have enough of that.

He was too sick to remain with us, though. One night he was sent to the hospital, where he was given blood, put in a taxi, and shipped back to the shelter. Still very sick, he was sent immediately back to the hospital. Again, he was given blood, placed in a taxi, and brought back to the shelter. After it happened a third time that night, we gave up and kept him.

We knew that Richard had family in town, but we had a difficult time reaching them. Stephen told me that Richard's father had not approved of his lifestyle and now wanted his son to live with its repercussions.

"But he's dying!" I said, unable to comprehend how a parent could cut off the relationship with his son.

"I know," replied Stephen, "but I've talked to him. It's no use."

Richard continued to grow sicker. He continued to make impossible demands upon Stephen and the staff. Whenever I saw him, it was usually because he had refused to take his medicine or go see his doctor. I would barge into the clinic and inform him that as long as he stayed in my shelter, he would play by my rules.

He would turn his head and say in a weak voice, "I'm not in the mood for company right now."

When it got to the point that he was throwing up several times a day and the hospital would still not keep him, it was the last straw. I had Richard moved to a nearby hotel. Stephen would attend to him there. After several days and dozens of bloody sheets, the hotel manager sent him back to the shelter and sent me a bill for the sheets.

One day his father called and asked for me. "How is he doing?" The voice was cold and formal.

"Not well. I can't keep him here."

"How long do you think he has?"

"I'm not a doctor! He's very sick. He throws up every day! He bleeds all over the bed. I have one hundred people in here every night and all of them are scared to check in. If it wasn't so cold out there, they certainly wouldn't be here at all. This situation is taking advantage of them!"

"His mother and I were thinking about coming to see him."

He did not appear to hear anything I said. They did come visit. It was quick. He did not say much to me when we met. Coming out of the clinic, he wiped tears from his eyes. They left without saying anything. When I went into the clinic, Richard told me that he did not feel like having company.

Several days later, his father called me again. Already angry, I asked if they were going to allow Richard to come home.

"Will you do me a favor?"

"What?"

"Call me when he dies." Then he hung up.

I held the phone a long time, staring into the buzzing receiver, trying to understand. How could a father concede his son's death before it had occurred? What had happened that was bad in the past? Didn't he understand that if he didn't make peace with his son now, there would never be another chance?

That night, Richard's illness grew even worse. We again sent him to the hospital. To our amazement, he was admitted. We learned that when AIDS patients are close to death, the hospital would keep them. The next day, however, he was back in the shelter. When I got there, demanding to know the hospital's excuse this time, I was told that Richard had checked himself out. He told Stephen that we were the only family he had left. I didn't know how to respond.

A few days later, Richard died. It did not happen at the shelter. We had to send him back to the hospital. This time, he was simply too sick to check himself out. The funeral was held on a bright sunny afternoon. The entire shelter staff attended, as did many from his church and his entire family. There were numerous flower arrangements around the coffin. The minister whom Richard had interrupted so many times spoke of love and forgiveness in life and in death. Standing beside me, Stephen recognized his own end, hugged me, and cried. Richard's father stood in silence.

As the service concluded and the coffin was lowered into the ground, no one moved. The three grave diggers moved into place, picked up their shovels, and began heaping loads of red clay into the plot. Everyone watched until they had finished. When they left, Richard's father walked to the car, got in, and drove away.

> *. . . they cried with a loud voice, "O Sovereign Lord, holy and true, wilt thou refrain from judging and avenging our blood on those who live on the earth?"*
>
> —Revelation 6:10

> *He came therefore again to Cana of Galilee. . . . And there was a certain royal official, whose son was sick at Capernaum. . . . The royal official said to him, "Sir, come down before my child dies."*
>
> —John 4:46ff.

God of life and death,
I do not understand a relationship
so torn and fragmented that forgiveness cannot occur,
healing cannot begin,
and life cannot flicker in the face of death.
I know how badly people can hurt one another.
Men betray their wives,
children offend and dishonor their parents,
and friends inflict wounds upon each other that never mend
and leave scars that never go away.
Why do we not see past the scars,
concentrating on them instead of the person?
Why do we not seek to heal the spirit
when we cannot heal the body?
Why do we not leap across the fragmented canyons
of broken relationships?

Why do so many family trees have broken branches?
Give me the strength to look beyond the scars
and see the suffering still there
so that I can touch the wound
and love the person.
Give me the wisdom to understand forgiveness
when I am confronted with it.
Give me the strength to represent you
when your presence is not wanted
and your healing is not desired.

— 20 —

Old Clothes

LAST NIGHT I was able to go to church for the first time in quite a while. It was a midweek prayer service that started with a fellowship meal, followed by several thousand announcements, a committee report on the status of other committees, and finally a sermon on what the pastor would do if he were a typical church member. I have found I enjoy this service much more than the Sunday morning one. The informality appeals to me.

It had been a difficult week. As always there were more homeless than we had space for. Volunteers were sparse so staff were doubling up and performing extra duties. The meeting of the board of directors had centered upon finances and, because contributions had been down, the budget was tight and most of the staff were left wondering if they would have jobs next month. It all left me feeling as though the bucket I used to empty the ocean was in danger of being repossessed because the payment was in default. I was depressed and wondering if what I did made any real difference in the world.

I was hoping a dose of church fellowship would help me forget I was a minister for a while. I was ministered out. I did not want to hear another person tell me her problems. I could not bear to see another homeless child sleep on the floor. The thought of another homeless person with AIDS needing housing because the hospital would not admit him made me furious. I was sick of telling people how to get off the streets and into their own apartments only to see them repeat the same actions that led them to the streets in the first place. I did not want to ask anyone else for money or time or talents. All I did want was to be accepted, affirmed, and allowed to participate quietly in a church service where I would receive just enough strength to return to the shelter tomorrow.

Well aware that such preoccupation with my own needs and desires was not good and not biblical either, I told myself that we all have to be selfish and think about ourselves sometimes. It is a safety mechanism. Sometimes I simply had to forget everyone else's needs and concentrate on my own.

After fixing our plates, my family moved to a far corner and sat next to some friends. I sat down, took a long breath, looked at the food, and realized I couldn't possibly eat. I was too tired. People called my name, extending greetings and saying how nice it was to see me again. Scanning the fellowship hall, I saw him.

He was old and feeble. His cane rested next to his chair. His glasses, bifocals, rested on the very tip of his nose, as if they were about to fall into his plate of fried chicken, yellow rice, peas and salad. His bald head gleamed underneath the bright light over him. He raised his hand, waved, and called me by name.

I didn't know him, although he obviously knew me. In a soft voice he called across the room and asked if he could see me for a moment. I walked over and knelt by his chair. Another friend I had not yet seen slapped my back and we exchanged jokes. The old man who knew me smiled and waited silently until I finished. When I looked at him again his mouth was full of chicken and I had to wait until he chewed and swallowed.

He looked at me and asked in a harsh way, "Why don't you put a sign up in front of the shelter?"

Caught off guard since I had not expected any shop talk here, my defenses flew into place. I explained the shelter's name was above the front door and that city codes probably prevented a sign from being placed next to the sidewalk.

"I drove up and down that street looking for it," he mumbled. "Must have spent an hour looking for that place."

I quickly told him exactly where it was. When he nodded and indicated he knew where it was, I grew silent and hoped that was all he wanted.

"I have some clothes that I was trying to bring you. All the folks in my neighborhood give me what they don't want or can't get rid of at their yard sales. I've got a small box in the trunk of my car. They've been there a month now. Can you get them before you leave?"

I told him I could and walked back to my family. After I told my wife what he wanted, she sighed and commented that I couldn't even get away from it here. I picked at my food and restlessly sat through the rest of the service.

After the service concluded, I stood around waiting for my wife to finish talking. All I wanted now was to go home. Then he caught my eye again. I walked over and followed as he slowly went outside. A one-minute walk took five. When he opened his trunk, I picked up the small box of clothes. He talked about how difficult it was for him to drive and how he had nowhere to go anyway as his family was all dead. He reminded me to send him a receipt for his taxes as he stuffed the name and address into my shirt pocket. I smiled, thanked him, and told him I would make sure he got it.

As I carried the box across the crowded parking lot, my family caught up and fell into step beside me. My two-year-old daughter ran along crying for Daddy to hold her hand. I couldn't because I was carrying another box of old clothes to the shelter.

> *"We must work the works of him who sent me, while it is day; night comes, when no one can work. . . . "*
>
> —John 9:4

God who offers rest for the weary,
where do I draw the line
between my personal life and needs
and the never-ending needs
of the world around me?
Sometimes
I am too tired
to help others direct their gifts to the poor.
I do not want to be nice
to someone who is donating something
out of convenience
more than out of conviction.
I want to get in my own car,
roll up the windows,
and withdraw into my own cave.
I want to be selfish,
and I do not think there is anything wrong with this.
I know the Bible tells me to be a cheerful servant,
but I'm tired.
So I will not ask for forgiveness.
Neither will I be especially cheerful
when I serve.
I pray that you understand.
And I pray
that you make anyone else who needs to
understand too.

— 21 —

Sleeping Over

JAMES IS IN THE NINTH GRADE. Every morning, like children across the country, he gets up, eats his breakfast, brushes his teeth, and runs to catch the bus to school. He dresses like most of his peers, blue jeans, T-shirts with something on the front, and high-top tennis shoes with the colorful laces left untied. His books are thrown across his shoulder in a knapsack. The only real difference between James and his classmates is that he is homeless. It is not home that he returns to after school, but the shelter. He does not go to his room to do his homework, but to the dining hall with all the other children who are school age. Most days, he must hurry to finish. Once the shelter is opened and a hundred other home-less men, women, and children check in, it will be much too noisy to concentrate on his assignments.

Like everyone at school, James quickly made friends, and it came as no surprise when he announced one afternoon that he had been invited to sleep over at a friend's house. Since he lived at a shelter, however, he first had to obtain special permission from his caseworker, which was quickly granted. As the special day approached, everyone caught some of James's excitement.

On Friday he took extra clothes in his schoolbag and told us he would see everyone on Saturday. Several recalled how special it had been in their childhood to sleep over with a friend for the first time. James's invitation seemed to remind us all of our own childhood. It is unusual, after all, for homeless children to be invited to sleep over with a friend. It is even more unusual for a homeless child to accept such an invitation. Most are painfully aware they are homeless, living in a shelter, with a parent or parents who are unemployed or underemployed. Then again, James was an exception in many ways. He was a good student. He had become friends with many of the staff and volunteers, not exhibiting the normal introverted social life of a homeless child. Everyone was confident James would fit in with the family hosting him and that he would have a good time as well as a much-needed break from the shelter.

Like most mothers, Rachel worried about her son. This was his first time away from her. Their relationship had been one of stress for several weeks. In addition to being a student, James had to baby-sit his two-year-old sister every afternoon so Rachel could work. It was only a part-time job, but it did provide some income. She was afraid he would come back wanting toys the other boy had, and she knew there was little chance of getting him any. Even in a shelter, the bond between a mother and her son can be strong.

Late Saturday morning, the car pulled into the shelter parking lot. James and his friend were playing in the back seat. The woman driving eyed the building with eyes full of suspicion. The two boys ceased playing as James quietly collected his things. The other boy paused to view the shelter. He looked confused. James moved slowly as though he did not want to get out of the car. No one spoke when he opened the door.

Standing outside, James softly thanked them for letting him spend the night. He said he really enjoyed it. He hung his head down as he spoke and the mother looked as though she was straining to hear his words. Her eyes continued to dart from James to her own son and back to the shelter. Embarrassed, James did not move away from the car door, but continued to gaze into the vehicle. Finally, the door was shut and the car quickly pulled out of the parking lot and sped away. James watched until it was out of sight. His knapsack hung by his side. Slowly picking it up, he turned and faced the shelter. Tears rolled down his face. Each step he took was filled with pain as he made his way back, not to home, but to a place he stayed with his mother and sister. Before coming inside, he wiped his eyes dry and then he ran to his room.

After that, James did not seem to talk as much. He continued to do his homework and baby-sit his sister, but it was more like a routine now. He never really told anyone if he had had a good time or not. After a while people quit asking. If anyone ever invited him to spend the night again, he must have told them no, because he never slept over with anyone else again.

> *Then children were brought to him that he might lay hands on them and pray. The disciples rebuked the people, but Jesus said, "Let the children come to me, and do not hinder them; for to such belongs the kingdom of heaven." And he laid his hands on them and went away.*
>
> — Matthew 19:13–15

God who loves the children,
why are there so many in this world
who do not have homes,
whose friends are fleeting,
who have to endure unnecessary pain before their time?
It is easy to blame adult males for being homeless.
We believe they could work if they were not lazy.
It is easy to blame adult females for being homeless.
We believe they can work too.
Or we believe they could find someone to care for them,
since they obviously cannot care for themselves.
But how can we blame children, Lord?
Through no fault of their own,
they find themselves homeless.
Saddest of all,

many do not really understand what being homeless means
until they are painfully reminded
when they are simply trying to do
what all the other children do.
When the realization comes,
more pain than most adults can bear
is laid upon their shoulders,
and we see their knees buckle under the weight,
as they continue their walk toward adulthood.

— 22 —

Used Food

I DON'T LIKE FAST FOOD RESTAURANTS. Like most Americans I fall captive to their convenience, and my children's minds have been kidnapped by their television commercials. But I resent them. One of the problems with the world is "coffee in a cardboard cup." (This is the name of a song that perfectly describes what I am talking about.) Meals should be a time when we slow down, have a conversation with a friend, and truly enjoy the food. Fast food places deal in volume, getting as many customers as possible in and out as quickly as possible. Their public relation campaigns lead us to believe everything about our lives would be brighter if we would only eat their hamburgers.

A fast food establishment sits across the street from the shelter. Too many days, I find I am too busy to go out for lunch and I do not eat what has been donated to the homeless, so I walk across the street, purchase a stamped-out sandwich, bring it back to the office, and pray it is nutrition I am getting. Today was one of those days.

Carrying my paper bag full of wonder back with me, I passed the drive-through menu and loudspeaker. Out of the corner of my eye, I saw a little girl standing beside the speaker and talking at it.

117

"I'll have two double cheeseburgers," she said as she danced in the spot where cars drive through, "and french fries and. . . . "

She went on ordering, but no one inside was paying attention to her. She was not in a car. An old man sat on the curb beside her, looking sad and forlorn. He wore a tattered coat and there were holes in the bottom of his shoes. Standing behind the outdoor menu was a woman dressed in dirty clothes observing two small children running around the parking lot. One was a boy, about ten. The other, a girl about four, was dirty and thin. Her bright eyes were huge, still undaunted by the poverty she lived in. When her sister placed the imaginary order, the little one would look in excited expectation for the speaker to respond. When it did not, she would look back to her older sister, not understanding why.

Someone called my name as I continued walking. It was another of the shelter's guests. I recognized her only because I had just finished helping her with something. Mrs. Akens was thin, dirty, and covered with buttons she had collected. Some were anti-apartheid, some were from a recent political campaign, and some were religious. She stuttered when she talked, but unlike many, she looked directly into my eyes throughout the encounter.

"I was leaving when I saw this poor child," she began, "talking to that stupid machine. Do you know what just happened?"

I told her that I did not.

"Well, her mamma here asked the machine if the people inside knew a place where her family could go. She told 'em they did not have a place to sleep tonight. Do you know what those stupid people said? They said they didn't know of no place around here. Imagine that, right across the damn street and they don't know."

It was difficult to believe. Like many who run restaurants, these people did not like it when the shelter opened across the street from them. While the homeless proved to be great customers, buying countless cups of coffee and lunch diets of little more than hamburgers, they did not want to cater to this kind of people.

They went so far as to offer police officers free lunches in return for running the vagrants out. It was not so much a case of not knowing where the shelter was, but of wanting to believe it was somewhere else.

The little girl stopped talking to the machine, walked over to her mother, hugged her, and apprehensively looked at me. The other children did the same. The old man stood up, spit on the pavement, and walked away. He was not a part of their family. I was introduced as the man who runs the shelter and asked if I could talk with the woman. The bag I was holding suddenly felt as if it weighed a ton.

I explained I might need to send them somewhere other than the shelter and it might save them steps if I learned what they needed now. Mrs. Akens did not like my answer, but grew silent anyway.

In a soft voice, filled with embarrassed pain, the mother told me they had no place to go. They had slept outside the night before. I interrupted, told her I understood, and took them to the shelter with me. Inside the crowded waiting room, they sat until I made sure there were leftovers from lunch. It was food that had been donated by a church group that had hosted a special event. They had purchased more than they needed and had given the leftovers to the shelter. This food had already been used twice and would not be used again. I found some and I had them follow me to the lunch room. The mother told me she didn't have to eat. Her son, trying to be the man of the family, immediately said he wasn't hungry either. I asked him if he was sure and he said he was. The baby told me she was hungry. The older girl nodded she was too. I encouraged them to go ahead and eat while I checked on what kind of space was available. As I walked away, the little boy asked for a plate too.

In the office I learned there was no room. A quick check showed the other shelters were also filled. I hate the feeling that comes when this situation arises. It reminds me of the Christmas story. Mary and Joseph are looking for a place to stay and the innkeeper tells them he has no room. I identify with the innkeeper too much. At least he had the luxury of offering a barn out back. Then the phone calls came and I was sidetracked. By the time I was free, I learned another of the staff had told them we were full and they would have to find shelter elsewhere.

I ran through the building looking for them, but they were nowhere to be found. I looked outside, across the street, at the fast food place, but there was only the old man seated underneath the outdoor menu. The family was nowhere to be found. I wanted to see them again. I would have found some space. I won't turn children down. There are too many on the streets at night, listening to their stomachs, growing up before they are supposed to, sleeping when they can and dreaming of clowns who offer them double cheeseburgers and fries.

If you oppress poor people, you insult the God who made them; but kindness shown to the poor is an act of worship.

— Proverbs 14:31

And she gave birth to her firstborn son and wrapped him in swaddling clothes, and laid him in a manger, because there was no room for them in the inn.

— Luke 2:7

God of the hungry and the full,
why are there so many
who live their days wishing for food
and their nights dreaming of it?
There is so much in the world
no one has to go without.
Is it because there are so many
who see hunger only as a means to profit?
What of the mother who does without,
teaching her children to be filled with pride
rather than good things to eat?
What of all the ones

who have more food than they will ever need,
donating what is not used
so they will not have to worry about leftovers?
I should not criticize, Lord.
I'm glad they give used food to the shelter,
but I wonder about the people who are left over
when the food is gone.

— 23 —

A Deadly Dream

IT WAS A TENSE TIME for Martin Luther King, Jr.'s, annual birthday celebration. A recent bombing in Alabama had shocked many, but the mail bomb that killed a local lawyer and city alderman threw the celebration into chaos. I had met the attorney because of shared interest in the homeless problem in our community. The day he was killed, I was returning from a weekend away to celebrate my wedding anniversary. I tuned the radio to the local news, and a reporter presented the sketchy events. It happened in his office a few days before Christmas. I could think of many other city leaders someone might want to kill, but not him. He was kind, gentle, and full of passion for the poor.

The Economic Opportunity Authority sponsors an annual celebration for Martin Luther King's birthday. Two weeks after the murder of our alderman, fear was prevalent as a crowd much smaller than in previous years gathered in the small cafeteria. Police officers stood at the door, lined the aisles, and took up an entire row of seats. Nervously, I walked toward the seat at the head table designated for the keynote speaker.

Before I stepped onto the platform, one of the police grabbed my shoulder and told me not to worry. In addition to the uniformed officers present, there were several plainclothes detectives. There was a crowd of perhaps fifty; this meant there was probably a police officer assigned to every individual brave enough to attend. I did not find his assurances comforting.

No politicians chose to attend this year. Theo, who often jokes he is my only black male friend, told me they were too scared to come. Who could blame them though? We had all begun to feel smug and comfortable with how far we had come since the days of the civil rights movement. We were supposed to be past being frightened whenever blacks and whites chose to gather together. We felt racism was an issue that no longer merited much concern. To be sure, we knew there were people who still did not accept the concept of equality, but we had convinced ourselves that the days of murder were over. These recent killings painfully reminded us, however, that we had not come as far as we thought.

It was hard not to be nervous sitting there. My leg shook off the tension as the time for my speech drew closer. The police officers continued to move around, suspiciously eyeing the crowd. Those in attendance knew they were being watched and tried to act normal.

In the end, everything came out fine. The speech went well. Remarks were made by the few community leaders who were there. Everyone stood, locked hands, and sang "We Shall Overcome." Obviously not used to singing in public, the police officers shifted from one foot to the other. As soon as the benediction was given, the crowd immediately fled to the safety of their automobiles. Before turning the key, it dawned on most that their cars may have been bombed. Relief filled the faces of many when their vehicles started with no explosion. I returned to the shelter, sad to know how violent the world can still be. I remember thinking, as I drove back to the shelter, just how deadly Martin Luther King, Jr.'s dream could be for those who sought to live it out.

A few days later, at a family dinner, one of my uncles approached and asked how the speech went.

"Did you know the one that was killed?" he asked.

I said I did and went on to say how much I appreciated the alderman and how senseless his murder had been.

"At work the other day," he said, "I heard some of the guys calling you a stupid nigger lover. I told them to shut up — it was my nephew they were talking about."

"He's still a stupid nigger lover," they responded.

"What did you say?" I asked, realizing for the first time that the things I did affected my family.

"I told them you were not stupid," he blandly replied.

It took me a moment to catch the joke. When I did, he placed his arm over my shoulder and told me how proud he was.

But let justice roll down like waters, and righteousness like an ever flowing stream.

— Amos 5:24

For he is our peace, who has made us both one, and has broken down the dividing wall of hostility. . . .

— Ephesians 2:14

God of all people,
black and white,
rich and poor,
male and female,
old and young,
why are there still so many divisions in the world?
We have come so far,
able now to communicate with anyone in the world,
to see on television other people in other lands,
to hook our computers to theirs.
We know more than we have ever known,
gathering information from the farthest stars,
scooping mud from the bottom of the deepest sea,
learning all we can about the world around us.
We spend more time now

exploring ourselves,
talking with counselors and in support groups,
identifying those things
that make us who we are.
We know almost everything now.
Since we began eating from the tree of knowledge,
we know the difference between good and evil.
We know almost everything now, Lord,
except how to love
one another.

— 24 —

The Liberation of a Dream
(Isaiah 58:4–8)

AMERICA PAUSES ANNUALLY to celebrate a holiday that provides us the opportunity to remember the only *major* prophet that our country has ever produced. (To be sure, America has produced several "minor" prophets — Harry Emerson Fosdick, Clarence Jordan, Walter Rauschenbusch — but, alas, one of the problems of a minor prophet is that only a minority remembers who you are.) Only Dr. King changed the course of an entire nation.

While I have always respected, admired, and agreed with what Dr. King said and did, I am afraid that I never really participated in his holiday. I justified this by claiming that Dr. King would prefer that people work for the cause of justice, in my case with the homeless, rather than taking a day off. I always understood and supported the black community's celebration of the holiday, but I managed to excuse myself from the celebration. But no more.

Last year the shelter closed on Martin Luther King, Jr.'s, birthday. It was a last-minute decision that evolved in the following way. My good friends at the Economic Opportunity Authority invited me to participate in the service at the civic center. Because I am a Southern Baptist minister, and because I am actively involved in the struggle for social justice, and because they needed someone who could read, I was asked to read the Old Testament Scripture. I considered several of the texts that Dr. King is known for, but finally settled upon a passage from the prophet Isaiah that seemed to sum up, for me at least, all the things that Dr. King stood for.

Hear the words of the prophet again:

> *"Behold, ye fast for strife and debate, and to smite with the fist of wickedness: ye shall not fast as ye do this day, to make your voice be heard on high. Is it such a fast that I have chosen? A day for a man to afflict his soul? Is it to bow down his head as a bulrush, and to spread sackcloth and ashes under him? Wilt thou call this a fast, and an acceptable day to the Lord?*
>
> *"Is this not the fast I have chosen? To loose the bonds of wickedness, to undo the heavy burdens, and to let the oppressed go free, and ye break every yoke? Is it not to feed the hungry, and to bring the poor that are cast out to thy house? When thou seest the naked, that thou shalt cover him. . . . Then shall thy light break forth as the morning, and thine health shall spring forth speedily; and thy righteousness shall go before thee; the glory of the Lord shall be thy reward."*
>
> — Isaiah 58:4–8

The verses sum up everything that Dr. King struggled for. After last year's celebration, I was amazed at the number of people who called me wanting to know what book of the Bible they were in. I was reading a book by the black feminist writer Alice Walker at the time. As a white male, I found myself in a mood very close to repentance for all the oppression that my particular classification of humanity had built for other brothers and sisters.

During those months I had developed a close friendship with several blacks with whom I work. One of them had given me a crash course on what it is like always to be "on" when she is in public because she must "represent her race." We were at a conference in Washington, D.C. (It always amazes me that conferences dealing with the homeless take place in a Hyatt or a Hilton.) On the way to a meeting, I slid down a banister railing and tried to get her to. After she explained all the reasons why she could not, I found myself becoming very sensitized to her struggle. We could not act, to use Dr. King's words, like two children of different color in the same playground. My playground proved to be much larger than hers. I am still afraid that her struggle is not yet our struggle and it makes me sad that friends always have to be on guard.

Because of such feelings, I resolved to celebrate Dr. King's birthday and close the shelter office. Early Monday morning, I loaded my children into the car to take them to the parade. As we drove downtown, they told me what they knew of Dr. King. I was proud of how much they knew. At the same time I recalled my own struggle to overcome my prejudice growing up during the 1960s. My memories carried me back to the night that Dr. King was killed. I was a child, but I vividly recall my father rushing in, scared to death that the violence in the streets would reach our home in the suburbs. He threw a tract on the kitchen table. The pamphlet expressed the sorrow of the black community at the loss of the prophet. I remember thumbing through it and catching some of his fear.

At the parade, my children and I watched the celebration. As the floats and cars came by, I realized that there were only a handful of white people present. I had already noticed that no white churches seemed to be represented in the parade, while nearly every black church was. I wondered why my own church was not involved.

I began to recall all that I heard white people say over the days leading up to the holiday. Much was not kind. Many comments totally disavowed the holiday. While we pretend that racism is behind us now and that only some crazed nut would send bombs and murder innocent people through the mail, most of us know better. Too many people, both white and black, are as scared and ignorant as they were in the 1960s. For appearance' sake, we keep our racial feelings to ourselves.

Back home that night after the parade, I reread some of Dr.

King's sermons and was moved again by his powerful words. I remember how ashamed I felt that my own race chooses to view the holiday from a racial rather than a humanitarian perspective. To be sure, there are exceptions, but too many people fail to see that Martin Luther King, Jr.'s birthday is as much a religious as a national holiday. It is time that we move beyond approaching Dr. King's birthday from so shallow a base. It is a time of year for all of us, male and female, black and white, slave and free, to renew ourselves with the dream that Dr. King dared to dream!

Something has happened to that dream, though. It was a dream rooted in biblical principles, an American dream that calls for all men and women to be able to fulfill their potential. To hear some people talk, the dream today is little more than a justification to do whatever they please. Our country now has a runaway American dream that leads all people to live so beyond their means that we become possessed by our possessions and consumed by our consumerism. Our dream is no longer rooted in the biblical principles of peace and justice, but in a circus of vanity that leads individuals to demand more and more rights for themselves and give less and less thought to the poor and the outcast.

Dr. King's dream has been captured through the years and is being held captive by people who, for perverted reasons, choose oppression to freedom. His dream has been kidnapped so that we give charity and not companionship to the poor. We have redefined Dr. King from prophet to black activist who deserves a black holiday to be celebrated by mostly black people. It is time that the dream be taken back from the people who use it to justify their own goals and given to the population at large — all of us, male and female, black and white, slave and free.

Will D. Campbell, a friend of Dr. King when Will was the troubleshooter for the World Council of Churches, once told the story of how the evil of racism must be dealt with by all people, but especially the white community. Will was scheduled to appear on a Nashville radio call-in show. As he was driving to the station, Will tuned in so that he could get a feel for the type of people who called in. Most of the calls concerned an appearance on the night before by a country singer. According to Will, the star had cursed on the show and the majority of the callers were expressing outrage at the language he had used. Will began to form a plan.

When he arrived, he was introduced as a Baptist minister who had worked in race relations during the 1960s as a writer and minister-at-large since. The first call was from an elderly lady who wanted to know how Will, as a Baptist minister, felt about the language that Charlie Daniels had used the night before.

"Well," said Will, "I don't know what he said so I couldn't really say. If you want me to comment, tell me what he said and I'll comment."

"Oh, Reverend," the caller said, "I am a Christian lady and do not use that kind of language."

"Well ma'm," continued Will, "I respect that. I can understand how you would not want to use those words, being a Christian and all, but I can't comment on what Charlie Daniels said unless I know the words. I'll tell you what, I'll say the baddest words that I know and when I get to the ones that he said, you just let me know, then I can comment."

The caller nervously cleared her throat. The technician in the glass booth put his finger on the four-second delay button. The show's host began to gulp down her glass of water.

"Are you ready?" Will asked. "Nigger. Is that one?"

Confused, the caller said no.

"AIDS," continued Will. "Is that one?'

There was no response, but the technician smiled as he moved his finger away from the button.

"Poverty? Racism? Sexism?" continued Will.

A very loud click was heard as the caller slammed the phone. "Well," concluded Will, "those are the worst bad words that I can think of. I'm sorry that the caller hung up because somebody needs to be talking about those words, but if that's not what she's talking about I don't reckon I have anything to say." (A version of this story appears in Campbell's *Forty Acres and a Goat*.)

Dr. King's dream must be liberated, and I am afraid that the black community cannot set it free alone. It is not a dream only for black people, but one that the white world must also make our own. So I find myself thinking subversive thoughts. Liberate the dream. Let us form a resistance movement that seeks to prevent the dream from being little more than a tool for the status quo. Liberate the dream!

Let us resolve that all forms of racism, however subtle they may be, are challenged whenever we encounter them, are purged from our hearts and faced openly and honestly and as completely as we can. Let us liberate the dream!

Those of us who are losing faith in the progress made since Dr. King first dreamed, who find ourselves sinking into despair, doubt and hate, let us have renewed faith in the dream!

Those who have been hurt by the racism, both individual and corporate, that is still alive, who have been abused and broken, who have had our trust broken down and the defenses of hostility have turned us inward, let us liberate the dream and learn to love again!

Those of us who have lost faith in the organizations that have institutionalized the dream so that it seems more care is given to buildings than people and more attention is paid to numbers than individuals, let us liberate the dream! Let us rebuild the beloved community!

Those who are tired of playing the games of subtle racism, who are forced to pretend to be something other than who we really are, let us liberate the dream and strive to live out our potential!

Those who are depressed from the nuclear cloud that hangs overhead and from leaders who are warmakers, let us liberate the dream that calls for the lion to lie down with the lamb.

Those who cannot stomach a leader more interested in re-election than in community service, let us liberate the dream that calls for men and women who will lead us down the paths of righteousness.

Those of us who have known hunger and poverty and who

are tired of fighting losing battles against hunger and poverty, let us liberate the dream that reminds us of strength in numbers and unity in diversity.

Those of us who have been given much and do not need a dream to believe in because our bills are paid and strangers treat us with respect, let us liberate the dream that reminds us of our brothers and sisters who need our excess; let us become a part of the whole family of humanity.

Too much time has passed, my friends. The dream is not to be kept under a glass to be pulled out once a year, dusted off, admired and celebrated, and then tucked away until next year. Let us liberate the dream and make it one of the guides by which we live every day. Then, perhaps, future celebrations will look more like a family dinner than a political rally with extra security guards.

Let us begin now my brothers and sisters. Let us liberate the dream!

PART FIVE

Partners in Grace

NEVER KNOWING WHEN GRACE MAY OCCUR, most go through life assuming there is none. But grace is there if we can see it: The boss does not chew us out when we plainly messed up and deserve it. A lover does not kick us out when we have been unfaithful, but offers one more chance. The bank does not foreclose when the payment is late and gives us additional time. A teacher offers a make-up exam for extra credit when we failed the test. God forever gives us the chance to start over after the first beginning did not work out.

There is a catch. There always is. The catch of grace is you can never be certain when it is going to occur. It might, but it might not. When it does not, the world crashes at our feet and life loses its luster. When it does, however, and we recognize that, through no effort of our own, we have a second chance, we cannot help but giggle a bit, sigh out a thanks to God, and promise to do better next time. Grace is knowing that there is always a next time.

— 25 —

The Gift of the Poor

RAISING THE PUBLIC'S AWARENESS is one of the ongoing duties of operating a homeless shelter. Every day there is another church or civic organization to address; there are ladies' groups to meet with or public events to participate in. This particular Tuesday I was at the weekly meeting of the Rotary Club in the DeSoto Hilton Hotel. I was met by William, the chairperson of the Program Committee. He had called me several weeks earlier to invite me to their meeting. A brisk, formal, very businesslike man, he immediately began to tell me the format of the meeting, where I would sit, when I would speak, and at what time I had to be finished. After completing his rapid-fire instructions, he motioned me to follow as he led me past the registration desk to my seat at the head table.

The bell rang to call the meeting to order. Someone mumbled a prayer. Everyone recited the Pledge of Allegiance. The club president told us we could eat. This is a difficult time for me. I like to be in silence before speaking publicly, but usually find myself surrounded by my hosts and feel the obligation to participate in small talk. William was seated beside me. He had asked several questions to know how to introduce me, but was now concentrating on the meal.

"What do you do for a living?" I asked.

"I am in the chemical distribution business."

I am certain that I expressed some reaction. One of the things I had noticed since moving to South Georgia is the great amount of chemical dumping that occurs. This was the first time I had met someone that dealt with chemicals for a living.

"Do you dump chemicals?"

William continued chewing his food, but he put his fork down and folded his fingers and rested his chin against them in thoughtful consideration. He sat in silence for so long, I grew uncomfortable and felt that I had offended him. Slowly, he turned and studied me carefully for the first time. He cleared his throat and spoke to me the way a professor addresses a student.

"Every day, from the time that my feet hit the floor until the time they are placed under the covers again, I break the law."

A sense of righteous indignation began to swell inside me.

"But so do you," he quickly added.

"I beg your pardon," I questioned.

"So do you. You speed in your automobile. You park on someone else's time at the parking meter. You do not account for all your income at tax time. Everyone breaks the law. You see, the country we live in makes it so we cannot live and resist breaking the law. There are so many regulations in the chemical business, and in all walks of life, that one cannot help but break the law."

I had never heard such a confident argument. William picked up his fork again and resumed eating. I put my fork down and thought for a long time before speaking.

"I suppose the question should be do you intentionally break the law or has it become second nature to do so. I think that there is a difference."

Again William put down his fork, but before he had time to consider my response, the club president again rang the bell calling the group to order. The captain came to the platform and charged certain members a quarter or a dollar for some infraction of club rules. Announcements were made and William was called upon to introduce me. He did so in a very formal and brisk manner.

I spoke passionately on the need of the homeless to be in relationship. I believe the single greatest factor that keeps people homeless is their lack of supportive relationships. Should I lose my job, my wife and family are there to provide much needed emotional support and to cheer me on. The homeless have no such support. If the church would rediscover the words of Jesus that it exists for the sick and not for those who are well and be the family for the family-less, I do not believe that there would be a homeless problem in America.

After the meeting was over, several of the club members asked questions and stated how interested they were in the homeless issue, especially how it might affect tourism, the city's fastest growing segment of the economy. Suddenly, William stood before me.

Handing me one of his business cards, he said, "I am a very busy man. I work long hours each week. I am the chairman of my church's building committee and we are presently constructing a new sanctuary. I am involved in this, and several other civic clubs. I do not have a great deal of time. If you should ever face an emergency, however, one in which you have no other resource, you can call me."

As I stuck his card in my pocket, he hurried off. I felt that I had witnessed the finest brushoff I had ever seen. Collecting my materials, I returned to the shelter.

Several mornings later, William came to the shelter and asked if I had a few moments to talk. Inviting him into my office, I noticed that he carried one of my books with him.

"I was struck by several of the things that you said at the Rotary Club meeting. I am a religious man and a practical one. As I told you, I do not have a great deal of time. However, I would like to help."

We talked about volunteering, contributing money, and other ways in which he might become involved. He admitted that he was too busy for most of these options, so he wrote a check and left. Several days later, however, he returned.

"I find," he said, "that I cannot shake the feeling that I should be doing something. My plate is simply too full at the present time. Can you give me a little while to clean it before you let me know what I can do?"

"Jesus said that the poor will be with us always," I replied. "They are not going anywhere."

"Why do you think that? This is America. No one has to be poor."

"I believe that the poor are one of God's greatest gifts to us."

"Gifts?" William bellowed.

"You see, we have so much. When we accumulate so much money and so many things, I believe that we become more self-centered. We become possessed by our possessions and consumed by our consumerism. God gave us the poor so there would always be someone to focus our giving toward. They help us to get off center and fulfill the call to share. If they were not here as a constant reminder, there would be nothing to pull us out of ourselves."

William thought for a long time before he wrote another check and left. He told me that he would be back, but I found myself doubting it. His checks had come too easily. Americans have reduced charity to writing checks. It is a quick and painless way to make us feel we are supporting God's work, but it provides no real emotional investment and almost no time.

I was proven wrong. In the months that followed, William did clean his plate. He made time for the shelter. He set up additional speaking engagements for me. He gave more money. He volunteered his time for shelter-related projects. He became a member of the board of directors and the chair of the Fundraising Committee. He made himself constantly available to me as a source of support and encouragement. He became a good friend who never tires and who has never said no.

*But what do you think? A man had two sons, and he came to the first
and said, "Son, go to work today in the vineyard." And he answered,
"I will, sir"; but he did not do so. And he came to the second son and
said the same thing; yet he answered, "I will not"; but afterward he
regretted it and went. "Which of the two did the will of the Father?"*
— Matthew 21:28–31

God of opportunity,
I find that there are too many choices confronting me.
I must do my work,
make time for my family,
fulfill social obligations,
support my church,
and give my money.
My plate is too full!
I do not have the time or the energy
to do all the things that the Gospel calls me to do!
When is enough really enough?
On top of everything else
you confront me with the poor.
Their need never ceases.
Their presence is ever before me.
I do not know how to help someone
who is so different from me.
Why are they here?
I try to do my share; I am a good person.
Why should there be more opportunity to give to others
than there is desire to give?
I do not really want to involve myself with them,
but the call is quiet and persistent for me to do so.
Why did you cast your lot with the poor?
Why do you call me to do the same?
Understand, Lord, that I do not really want to,
but I will try.

— 26 —

Giving Thanks

ROGER IS THE DIRECTOR OF POTTER'S PLACE, a twelve-bed transitional facility for homeless persons who are trying to overcome an addiction to drugs and/or alcohol. He is a colorful character who talks like a sailor, has arms and legs covered with tattoos, and has done a bit of everything during the forty-two years of his life. Having survived four failed marriages, his own addiction to both drugs and alcohol, and several months of homelessness, Roger talks freely of the lessons learned from his experiences. Something of a salty philosopher, he once gave a definitive explanation of how relationships should be maintained.

Conversing with a friend who was in an on-again/off-again relationship, Roger encouraged her to draw a firm line and either get out of the relationship or treat it right.

"I was living under a bridge at the time," he began. "It was after my fourth marriage, and I was in pretty bad shape. I was missing my wife ... really I was missing being in a relationship, when this old guy told me something that put everything into perspective for me."

A funny and masterful storyteller, Roger had everyone's full attention.

"The old man told me, 'Listen, relationships are easy. You just have to know how to give thanks.'"

"What are you talking about? Giving thanks? Man, please," Roger asked him, but the old man continued undaunted.

"I'll tell you what I'm talking about. There is a street corner downtown. You go there and wait. Sooner or later a woman will approach you and ask if you'd like to have a relationship with her. If you want to, she'll ask you for some money. Nowadays, you can use a credit card."

"What has that got to do with anything?" Roger asked.

Still the old man continued. "The point is that you will give her your credit card and she will only charge the agreed upon price. Then you will have your relationship and when you finish, she will thank you and ask you to come back any time."

"I don't understand," Roger confessed. "What does a prostitute have to do with a real relationship?"

The old man commented on how dense Roger was. "Listen, if every relationship was approached that way, if every man and woman entered into a relationship that way, then there would not be as many failed marriages in this world. When did any of your wives ever hold the limit on your credit card and not go over the amount?"

Roger told the old man he had a point.

The old man continued to interpret his story. "And when was the last time a wife, after consummating the relationship she was in, thanked the man and then told him to come back any time?"

Roger told the old man he had another point.

"If people would just take the time to give thanks for the little things that make a relationship," Roger concluded, "and drew firm lines to remind themselves that relationships are gifts, then everybody who is in one would be a lot happier, and everybody who is not in one would be doing everything they could to get in one." We all laughed as Roger told his story. As the laughter faded, however, we could not but be struck by the truth of his words.

Be subject to one another out of reverence for Christ. Wives, be subject to your husbands, as to the Lord.... Husbands, love your wives, as Christ loved the Church and gave himself up for her.... He who loves his wife loves himself....

— Ephesians 5:21ff.

O God who gives the gift of relationships,
hear me pause to give thanks
for the abundance of friends that I have.
My friends are a principal source
of encouragement,
affirmation,
and challenge for me.
Without them,
life would be too much of a struggle
for me ever to face alone.
Thank you for my spouse,
who is my best friend
and one of the greatest gifts
you have been gracious enough to bestow upon me.
Too often, O Lord,
I am not worthy of such a gift,
neglecting it
and treating it as I would something I deserved,
never taking the time to think
how empty my life would be
without the power of such a relationship.
You knew how lonely the struggle to live can be,
and so you had relationships in mind
when the world was founded.
Now, excuse me, Lord, I have thanked you enough
and it is time for me to thank my spouse.

— 27 —

The Ministry of Political Football

IT IS TOUGH being both a minister and a football fan. Inevitably the game I want to watch conflicts with a sermon I must deliver or a meeting I must attend. I am famous for sitting in my parked car outside the church I am to speak in, tuned to the radio until the last possible moment before rushing in to the pulpit. During the first hymn, the church's minister will lean over and ask me if I had any problems finding the church. Typically I respond by telling him what the score was when I left and he immediately understands. (I rarely encounter a female minister and always wondered if they would accept my response with similar understanding.)

I attend as many football games as possible. My son, Jeremy, and my brother, David, are my constant companions. Occasionally I can drag other members of my family along. We pack our lunches, secure the cheapest tickets, and celebrate our favorite team, the Georgia Bulldogs, with eighty thousand of our closest friends. When I relocated from Kentucky, where football season lasts three weeks and basketball season never ends, back to Georgia, where football almost lasts long enough, I was happy to be with people who understand that when St. Paul wrote, "Watch out for the dogs . . . " in Philippians, he was referring to the University of Georgia football team.

Another team I follow is the Georgia Southern Eagles. When the Bulldogs (the correct way to pronounce it is "Dawgs") are not playing, I try to attend the Eagles' games. Occasionally, some of the volunteers at the shelter share my enthusiasm for football. Richard, one of the members of the board of directors, has booth seats at all Georgia Southern games. From time to time, I am invited in. Watching a college football game from a private booth is a fan's ultimate dream. Regardless of the weather, it is always comfortable in a booth. Should you wish to participate with the crowd in cheering the team on, you only have to open the windows. Televisions broadcast other games of interest. Food is plentiful, drinks available, and rest room facilities handy in these private rooms where the view is impeccable. Once you watch a game from a booth, you are hopelessly hooked and long always to be allowed in.

Unfortunately for me, only people who have a lot of money have booths and only people who know people with money get invited to them on a regular basis. Since I work in a homeless shelter, most of the people I know well do not have much money. The money they do have, however, is spent freely on friends. Almost every day, contrary to the stereotype, a homeless person is wanting to buy me a cup of coffee. I am always amazed at how freely homeless men and women are willing to share their meager resources with me.

I always have a good time whenever I am invited into Richard's booth. To be sure, the football game is part of it, but more often than not I enjoy the reaction when the others in the booth meet me. It seems I always cause confusion. No one thinks ministers who work with the homeless can be football fans or are ever invited into private booths.

"So what do you do?" they ask.

"I run shelters for the homeless and for people who have AIDS," I reply and I love the response. Their heads jerk to the side and they view me with confused suspicion. If they have been using foul language, they immediately apologize. Often they recognize the name of the shelter or claim they have seen me on the news. Then I ask what they do.

Most are bankers, lawyers, businessmen, and politicians. Typically, the conversations are short. After finding out what I do, the majority seem to believe I will ask them for money or launch into a sermon. They suddenly have to go to the bathroom or freshen their drinks. I am not put off by these reactions, and I usually just concentrate on the game, which allows me to escape from the never-ending problems of the poor. Sometimes, however, people are really interested. It seems the most interest comes from the wives. Women prove they can express compassion anywhere, often wanting to know about the ministries and what they might do to help.

Those who intrigue me most, however, are the politicians. Many know me because those who work with the homeless follow politics, writing letters and attending meetings in an attempt to speak in behalf of those who will not, or cannot, speak for themselves. The mayor or congressman who sees me in the booth recognizes my face, but can't quite remember from where. When I speak, confusion fills their eyes and I can see them asking themselves what in the world I'm doing there. I attempt to utilize these opportunities, reminding our elected officials of the homeless, usually referring to some specific agenda we have recently communicated about. I doubt they really hear me, though. After all, I'm not supposed to be there.

Once one did ask me how a minister could attend football games and sit in a booth with people of means who spend more money on football than they give to church or charity. I told him when Jesus went to heaven, his last words to the disciples were to be his witness in Jerusalem and in all Judea and Samaria and to the end of the earth. I told him I had finally found the end of the earth. He looked confused.

All things are lawful for me, but not all things are helpful....
— 1 Corinthians 6:12

God of the fun times,
I thank you for the numerous opportunities
offered for me
to have meaningless fun.
I recognize, Lord, the many
who do not have the chance to play.
They are too busy working
or concentrating on simple survival.
Yet, you have given me
permission to not always be serious,
to get away from life's harshness
when I need to.
Help me, Lord,
always to know when I need to play
and when I need to quit.
Help me to take full advantage
of the gift of fun times
without becoming too preoccupied with them.
Help these times to refresh me
so that I can return
to the work at hand.
And never let me confuse
where I need to be placing my energy.

— 28 —

Token Prayers

I AM OFTEN ASKED to pray the invocation at public functions. Because I am a minister without a church, I somehow represent all churches. Also, because of my involvement with social issues, the prayers I am asked to deliver are to speak of whatever ill the gathering is addressing. I have been asked to pray for world hunger, homelessness, AIDS, housing, senior citizens, children at risk, racism, and world peace.

I do a lot of blessings too. At dinner meetings, someone will realize I am a minister before the meal and, at the last minute, I am asked to say grace. I enjoy these occasions, and I usually provide a lot more prayer than they really wanted. It is not that the prayers are long, most are not, but they are pointed. At a banquet I will pray for those who are not eating in the world tonight and ask forgiveness that we have more food than we could possibly eat and much of it will be wasted. At civic functions, I thank God for being the same yesterday, today, and tomorrow, because our political system cannot decide if it really wants to be one nation under God or not.

After the function some will approach me and say how much they were struck by my prayer. They want to know if I made it up on the spot. Some will ask where I learned to pray like that. And some will tell me they do not appreciate my preaching a sermon when I am supposed to be offering a simple prayer. When this happens, I tell them I was not talking to them anyway.

From time to time, however, I find a different level of prayer in my life. Words are of no use during these times. At the weekly noon Mass I attended at St. Martin's Church I discovered true prayers. I had begun attending Mass at a time in my life when I was spiritually dry. Like many, I was under the false impression that if I surrounded myself with spiritual things, they would rub off on me and I would be more spiritual. St. Martin's is a beautiful sanctuary filled with statues of apostles, saints, stained glass, and mostly empty pews. A wonderful old pipe organ plays throughout the service. I felt rested whenever I attended, so noonday Mass became a custom. I became friends with the priest and had lunch with him after Mass. (In turn, he made it his custom to have Wednesday night supper with my church.)

Attending services very different from those of my own tradition on a regular basis gave me the opportunity to memorize most of the liturgy. This meant I could participate in the service. Dutifully I would recite the responses with the rest of the congregation. When it came time for the congregation to partake of the Lord's Supper, however, I was left out. Respecting their tradition, recognizing myself as a Protestant, I would remain in my place, kneeling in thoughtfulness as the priest continued to pass out the body and blood of Christ for all who wished to come. I knew that if I walked the aisle, the priest would dispense the elements to me, but I rarely went. After the last person received the host, the priest would pause, look directly at me, his eyes filled with pain in recognition of the barriers of our separate traditions, and wait for just a moment to see if I were coming. This prayerful moment was pregnant with the understanding that the body of Christ is indeed broken in the world today.

The priest would slowly turn, return the uneaten bread to its proper place, and then wash out the last of the wine from the chalice. After pouring in more water, he would drink it, then, taking a cloth, wipe it dry. I took this to mean he was squeezing every drop of Jesus out of the cup because, God knows, we need all of Jesus we can get.

After the Mass, over lunch, we often talked about this moment. It was holy for us. While administering the duties of a priest, he saw a brother struggler who wanted Christ's presence as much as anybody, but whose tradition prevented his coming. As a fellow worshipper, I recognized how far we could go together, only to find there were some steps I could not take. These moments, we decided, represented everything it means to be a Christian in the world today. Wanting the same things, religious traditions often become stumbling blocks to true Christian community. The sense of expectation, missed community, and divine presence during these moments has been the most powerful I have ever felt.

Since those days, I find most of my prayers token ones, emphasizing my words instead of God's presence and the struggle for fellowship with brothers and sisters who are separated from me. One thing has remained with me, however. When I am invited to pray, regardless of where, I pause for a moment before starting, scan the faces of those around me, seeing who close their eyes and who don't, and become aware that the possibility exists for divine presence. I am sure that the presence is always there, but I am also certain that we do not always recognize it. When we do not, the prayers are token, and the words are more for our benefit than for anything else.

And when you pray, you must not be like hypocrites; for they love to stand and pray in the synagogues and at street corners, that they may be seen.... And in praying do not heap up empty phrases as the Gentiles do; for they think that they will be heard for their many words. Do not be like them, for your Father knows what you need before you ask him.

—Matthew 6:5ff.

Our Father who is in heaven,
and here on earth too,
waiting to be heard,
waiting to be seen,
as we say the words
and go through the motions we have learned,
break through to us somehow.
We are too busy praying
to really communicate with you.
Our prayers are monologues
and not dialogues.
I have too much I want to say
so that I do not take time to hear
what you want to say to me.
I do not sense your presence
when it passes by me.
Sometimes, though,
you get through to me.
I thank you for these times
and desire they happen more often,
but right now I am in a hurry.
I have to attend another banquet.
I have been asked to say grace.

— 29 —

The Gift of Children

IF GOD IS LOVE, then why are there so many hungry people in the world?

Jeremy, part-time theologian, part-time football player, and my full-time son, was asking another one of his questions. From time to time, something goes off in his head, causing thoughts much too deep for a twelve-year-old to develop. He always catches me off guard. Sometimes he will pick up whatever book I'm reading, thumb through it, sometimes reading the whole thing, and ask me what I think of it. Typically he responds with his own thoughts regarding liberation theology or the ramifications of racism on the federal budget crisis. I am convinced he is a forty-five-year-old growing backward.

At a time when I do not concentrate much on theology, he forces me to struggle with difficult concepts, to come up with words that a child can understand, to explain the concepts to him. He helps me to speak of theological concepts in language anyone can understand. Often Jeremy's topic arises at work and someone understands my explanation only because Jeremy provided me the opportunity for a trial run.

Kristen, on the other hand, is a radical waiting to grow up. She has never met a stranger, will give away everything she owns to whoever asks, and knows no fear. She loves to come to the shelter with me to be the secretary. Pushing people away from the phone when it rings, she has to be the one to answer it. I often tell people that Kristen is going to grow up and overthrow Third World dictators for a living.

Once when she was with me at the shelter, I was absorbed in the needs of a hundred different people. Kristen found a Spanish migrant worker sitting alone in the waiting room. No one spoke Spanish, so lost in his own world, he waited. She had taken one year of elementary school Spanish and knew, perhaps, three incomplete sentences. She spent the entire morning repeating them to him. Each time he would respond at length, just happy to have someone to talk to. Because of her attention, we were alerted to his needs to give him the assistance he required. Were it not for her, he would probably have sat alone for a long time. Kristen makes me see needs I often miss.

Chelsea, my two-year-old, demands that I come into her room each night when I come in from work. She has me sit at her tiny table and chairs so she can serve me an imaginary supper. Barring everyone else from the room, this is her time with Daddy. While this was fun and cute the first hundred times she did it, it has gotten old now. Most nights I have to make myself sit with her when I would rather fall on the sofa and not do anything for a while. When I do not go directly to her room, however, Chelsea grabs the leg of my pants and pulls me there. There is always time.

Each of my children refocuses my often distracted attention to new needs and revelations I would otherwise miss. Each brings a unique perspective to my life and whenever I am too busy to stop and listen to them, I miss messages from God.

But this is only half of how my children affect my ministry. There is also an indirect effect. Increasingly, the homeless population is made up of children. Every day at the shelter, I interact with these homeless children. I share their joys and their sorrows. I am a part of their lives. As I see them struggle, my children come to mind. Some balance is struck between these children and my children. When I see a homeless child crying because her mother is too busy looking for work to pay her any attention, I remind myself to spend time with Chelsea. When a volunteer calls to say he cannot come today to take a homeless boy to a ball game, I promise myself that I will take Jeremy to one soon. When a homeless girl plays in the yard with broken toys, I rush home that day to play with Kristen.

It is a strange gift. The plight of homeless children makes me more sensitive to my own family. Were it not that God knew exactly where I was needed, I doubt I would be much of a father.

Truly, I say to you, whoever does not receive the Kingdom as a child shall not enter it. . . .

—Mark 10:15

God of those who pledge to stay forever young,
thank you for the times
when I am allowed to see
through the eyes of children.
Often it drives me to my knees,
for it is only down there
that I can see the world
from their perspective.
It is a different view
from what I see
when I am on top.
Too often, God,
I spend too much time
trying to be on top
rather than trying to see things from below.
I should remember, Lord,
that the only time
that you saw things from the top
was when you hung from the cross.

— 30 —

Roll Away the Stone
(Mark 16:1ff.)

THERE HAVE BEEN TIMES when the capability of human beings to walk with their God has been an unmistakable example of what can be accomplished, an indisputable triumph of the Reign of God on earth. These times are, however, few in the history of the world. Nevertheless, we as Christians can find illustrations of what might be done when people finally reach the point where they are no longer willing to settle for the lives they find themselves living. When this decision is reached, great Christians have done great things with their God.

St. Francis walked away from the captivity of wealth and materialism to embrace the beauty of God's creation. Martin Luther stood up and told the church what it was in a successful effort to make it better. Gandhi looked at his country, knew that classism was wrong, and lived a life overcoming it. Dorothy Day saw hungry people around her, even as she was hungry, and began to feed others. Martin Luther King, Jr., saw this country not living up to its potential and sought to bring the nation closer to what its founders intended. Clarence Jordan left the security of being white and embraced his black brothers and sisters years before the civil rights movement began.

When the lives of these and other saints are examined, we discover that each of them knew the word of God and responded to that word. On occasion, these saints lustfully looked back to the security of what this life has to offer, but, in the end, they each rolled away the stone that stood in their way and acted the way Christ would have them.

Before we get too romantic about our saints and heros, however, it would be wise to pause and consider the struggle that made them so loved, or hated, by the church. Their struggles were real! The issues that they acted upon were not attractive causes for them. St. Francis really was a materialist and spent a lifetime overcoming materialism's captivity. Martin Luther was a part of the same church he was trying to reform. Dorothy Day was herself a mirror of the hungry and the lost she served. Martin Luther King, Jr., and Clarence Jordan both grew up as racists and struggled with racism throughout their lives. They were not so much dealing with world issues, or even biblical issues, as they were with their own weakness and sin.

When it came to faith, our saints and heros did not get to choose their battles. Their personal wars were chosen for them. They did nothing more, or less, than face up to their own weakness and sin. Because they were willing to do this, they found the pathway of Jesus the Christ.

To think we have the luxury of choosing our battles is the height of arrogance. Yet too many Christians are doing just that. Whenever we pick and choose our cause as a follower of Christ, we are probably picking the cause we are most comfortable with. This is not choosing to become a part of the Reign of God as much as opting to remain comfortable.

Some choose to fight for the rights of unborn zygotes when they are unwilling to fight for equal rights or civil rights. Others will choose to fight for a truer and deeper spirituality, but will not look at the righteousness of their own spirits. Many will choose to involve themselves with unpopular issues but are unwilling to involve themselves with unpopular people. Most often, we choose one battle so that we will not have to fight another. This is not the way those who would follow Jesus must act.

Will Campbell, in *Forty Acres and a Goat*, relates the story of the minister father of a little black girl who was one of nine to integrate a school. There had been a great many threats against both the school and the children.

"One of the children was the daughter of Pastor Kelly Miller Smith. Late one night, I sat with him in his study, peeking often through the window in a vigil against the threats to the building. After a long period of comfortable silence, I asked, 'Kelly, what if something happens to little Joy?'

"He moved the candle, the only light we had risked, closer to him and opened the Bible and began to read about Abraham being told by the Lord to take his little boy up on the mountain, tie him on a pile of wood, cut his throat, and burn him. He read a sentence and then talked about it.

" 'Take now thy son, thine only son Isaac, whom thou lovest, and get thee into the land of Moriah; and offer him there for a burnt offering upon one of the mountains which I will tell thee of.'

" 'You see, my brother, we don't even get to choose the mountain,' he said. 'God chooses the mountain. All we're asked to do is obey.'

" '. . . And Abraham built an altar there, and laid the wood in order, and bound Isaac his son, and laid him on the altar upon the wood. And Abraham stretched forth his hand, and took the knife to slay his son.'

"I thought he was going to cry as he half-closed the book. Instead he began to laugh.

" 'Will, we're talking about some mighty hard sayings. We're talking about faithfulness to Almighty God. The God of Abraham, Isaac, and Jacob. The God of my black mama and daddy in Mississippi and your white mama and daddy in Mississippi. If that God says we've got to do it, well, we've got to do it' " (p. 51).

When it comes to following God we do not get to choose the battles. We do not even get to choose the mountain. All we get to do is choose if we will obey or not. This is what made the saints and heros of our faith: They obeyed.

Where does this fact of faith leave us? How do we choose to follow God when we are forever choosing to do the things we are comfortable with? How are we to face the music that keeps us dancing a tune of falsehood and deception with ourselves and one another? How are we to obey when we are not even certain what the commands are?

The first step is to be honest with ourselves. Each of us is fully aware of the battle that looms before us. We know quite well where the mountain is that we, as individuals who would follow Christ, must climb. The first thing we need to do is face this fact.

For some this will mean acknowledging we are depressed and unhappy with who we are and what we are doing. It will mean admitting we are settling for less than is available to us. It will mean facing that we are afraid to have God make the choice for us.

For some it will mean admitting we are currently involved in the wrong battles. Before we can really be peacemakers we must make peace with ourselves and each other. We must learn how to forgive and to be forgiven. It means we must be initiators of love with people we often do not agree with. It also means saying and doing things we know the friends we are most comfortable with may not approve of.

For others it will mean no longer hiding behind the hallowed walls of privatism and individualism. It will mean fighting to open ourselves up to others instead of being cynical about them. It will mean that, instead of trying to see through others, we will see others through. It will mean admitting to others our own lust, greed, and shortcomings instead of trying to project ourselves as sinless. It means freely admitting we are ourselves sinners. It will mean choosing to fight the battle that will teach us to trust.

For some the battlefield lies more on the surface of our lives.

We are alcoholics, drug addicts, materialists, and gluttons. Finding Jesus will mean overcoming whatever prevents us from being ourselves.

For still others, the fight will be to overcome the lying, manipulation, and false images we utilize to keep ourselves safe and in control. We will have to learn how to go "spiritually streaking" through the relationships we are in. We will have to stand as we really are before others so that we can learn how lovely we are as ourselves and not as we think we have to be.

In the last chapter of the Gospel according to St. Mark there is a beautiful passage: "And when the Sabbath was past, Mary Magdalene, and Mary the mother of James, and Salome, bought spices, so that they might go anoint him. And very early on the first day of the week they went to the tomb when the sun had risen. And they were all saying to one another, 'Who will roll away the stone for us from the door of the tomb?'"

The real-life incidents behind the story are ones that we as followers of Jesus must never forget. The women thought Jesus was dead, killed as a religious fanatic and political criminal. His followers were outlawed, and these women were taking a great risk by publicly going to lay flowers on Jesus' grave. None of his disciples, the great men of the faith movement, would go with them. These women faced the fears the men would not. In fact, they faced their own worst fears, being arrested, mocked, raped, tried, perhaps even executed! As they faced these fears, they occupied themselves with the practical questions facing them. "Who will roll away the stone?" Certainly, they could not. They were just three women. Most would not even have made the effort to anoint the body, assuming the stone was unmovable.

Arriving at Jesus' tomb, however, they found it was already rolled away. How? Who did it? Was it the angel sitting on one side? Did Jesus break it down? Mark never really says. Perhaps it was the three women. It could be that with each step they took closer to the grave, and toward their own worst fears, was a force that inched the stone away from the tomb. Because they were willing to follow the love within their hearts at all costs, perhaps *they* rolled away the stone. Mark does tell us that when they arrived at the tomb, there was nothing, no rock, no arresting officers, not even death, to separate them from Jesus. This never would have happened had they not been willing to take those first steps out of the security of their homes early one morning.

You and I are faced with great stones that clutter the pathway of faith we wish to walk. These stones separate us from God and keep Christ dead for us. Like the three women and the saints and heroes of faith, we must ask: "Who will roll away the stone?" Who will help us to overcome the obstacles preventing us from being with God in the way we desire?

The answer, of course, is that we will — you and I! We will roll away the stone by obeying the God of Abraham, Isaac, and Jacob.

We roll it away by leaving the security of choosing our own battles to embark on the battlefields God has chosen.

We roll it away by confronting our own worst fears, sharing them with others and overcoming the prejudice we harbor.

We roll away the stone, you and I, for it was three women, not one, who moved the first one. Stones are moved away by bands of believers and not individual effort.

We roll away the stone, people of America, by foregoing nationalism and holding up God's values.

We roll away the stone, people of the church, by investing in people instead of buildings and song books.

We roll away the stone by saying to those who would prevent us, "Get out of the way, stones are falling and rocks are rolling, for I will let nothing stop me from being where my God wants me to be! God has chosen a place for me, and I will move anything in my way to get there!"

References Cited

Brown, Robert McAfee. *Creative Dislocation: The Movement of Grace.* Nashville: Abingdon Press, 1980.

——. *Unexpected News.* Philadelphia: Westminster Press, 1984.

Buechner, Frederick. *Wishful Thinking.* New York: Harper and Row, 1973.

Buscaglia, Leo. *Bus 9 to Paradise.* New York: William Morrow and Company, 1986.

Campbell, Will D. *Forty Acres and a Goat.* Atlanta: Peachtree Press, 1986.

Casanas, Joan. "The Task of Making God Exist." In *The Idols of Death and the God of Life,* edited by Pablo Richard et al. Maryknoll, N.Y.: Orbis Books, 1983.

Coles, Robert. *The Call of Stories: Stories and the Moral Imagination.* Boston: Houghton Mifflin, 1989.